# Oxford Secondary English

# Book 3

*John Seely*

and
*Frank Ash*
*Frank Green*
*Chris Woodhead*

Oxford
University
Press

Oxford University Press, Walton Street, Oxford OX2 6DP

*Oxford  New York  Toronto*
*Delhi  Bombay  Calcutta  Madras  Karachi*
*Petaling Jaya  Singapore  Hong Kong  Tokyo*
*Nairobi  Dar es Salaam  Cape Town*
*Melbourne  Auckland*

and associated companies in
*Beirut  Berlin  Ibadan  Nicosia*

*Oxford* is a trade mark of Oxford University Press

© Oxford University Press 1982

First published 1982
Reprinted 1982, 1983 (twice), 1984, 1985, 1986, 1987

ISBN 0 19 831137 0

There is a pupil's book and a teacher's book for each
year of *Oxford Secondary English*. The teacher's
book is an integral part of the course and contains
reproducible assignments on the material in the
pupil's book. Notes and advice for the teacher are
also included.

Printed in Great Britain by
Scotprint, Musselburgh

# Contents

# TWO SIDES TO EVERYTHING

TWO SIDES TO EVERYTHING

These photographs are grouped in pairs.
Between the pictures in each pair there are similarities
and differences. Discuss these: what do they tell us
about the people in the pictures?

# My busconductor

My busconductor tells me
he only has one kidney
and that may soon go on strike
through overwork.
Each busticket
takes on now a different shape
and texture.
He holds a ninepenny single
as if it were a rose
and puts the shilling in his bag
as a child into a gasmeter.
His thin lips
have no quips
for fat factory girls
and he ignores
the drunk who snores
and the oldman who talks to himself
and gets off at the wrong stop.
He goes gently to the bedroom
of the bus
to collect
and watch familiar shops and pubs passby
(perhaps for the last time?)
The sameold streets look different now
more distinct
as through new glasses.
And the sky
was it ever so blue?

And all the time
deepdown in the deserted busshelter of his mind
he thinks about his journey nearly done.
One day he'll clock on and never clock off
or clock off and never clock on.

**Roger McGough**

| Questions to think and talk about | | |
|---|---|---|
| | 1 | What has changed the bus conductor's way of looking at things? |
| | 2 | In what ways does he see things differently? |
| | 3 | What has he always got at the back of his mind? |
| | 4 | Suppose you were in the same situation as the bus conductor. What parts of your life would take on new importance? |

# Circles

The white man drew a small circle in the sand
   and told the red man,
   'This is what the Indian knows,'
   and drawing a big circle round the small one,
   'This is what the white man knows.'

The Indian took the stick
   and swept an immense ring round both circles:
   'This is where the white man and the red man
   know nothing.'

**Carl Sandburg**

| | |
|---|---|
| **Questions to think and talk about** | 1   What does this poem mean? |
| | 2   Can you think of people who think like the white man? |
| | 3   Do you ever feel like the white man? |
| **Writing** | 1   Think of an occasion when something has happened to make you look at things differently, or to see something for the first time. Write about what happened and how you felt about it. |
| | 2   Choose a person whom you often see but have never really thought about. Think carefully about that person for the first time, and imagine what his or her life is like. Write about it. |
| | 2   You have been involved in an accident and, as a result, have to spend two weeks with your eyes bandaged up. Describe your first day up and about but unable to see. |

# The accident

Grandma used to say how cheerful I was, continually busy and knocking about, a handful of such brazen curiosity that I'd take some looking after.

5 I ran out of her gate one day while they were drinking tea and eating cake. Across the road by the kerb was a dark green motor van and I opened the door without thinking. Inside I found a new world of leather upholstery and dials, handles and knobs, as well as a monstrous wheel. Standing up I could look out of the wide front window and see down the sloping road. I

10 was strong enough to pull the door shut after me, and then found some force to grip another handle that suddenly fell forward with a clatter, causing the flesh of my palm to ring as it hit its limits somewhere forward. A rumble under the whole car told me all was not right with the world, and standing

15 straight I saw my grandad's brick wall sliding backwards along the car. Then another house was in view, and, full of terror, I dropped into a bundle on the floor and cried out for my mother.

The car made ominous bounces down the road, ran across a junction at the bottom, and buried itself in a tall privet hedge,

20 grinding its side against a concrete lamp-post. A man came running, and when the door opened I felt a solid hand thumping at my head, and heard a voice calling me all the bad names that came to it. I cried, and thought my more-or-less pleasant world was coming to an end. My mother must have

25 been told what was happening, for I heard her curses as she began bashing the man at any part of his body she could reach. Grandma pulled me out and soothed me, praising God I hadn't been killed, and shouting against stupid dead-heads who left their cars by the roadside with open doors, and threatening to

30 get the police and have the bewildered culprit sent down for murder and kidnapping.

But the man was in tears, because he'd saved up half his life to get a little van to take his wife and kids along the Trent for fresh air at weekends. He'd polished it faithfully every week,

35 fed it with oats and water like a true yeoman of England grooming his horse, and now this act of God in the shape of the Devil's imp had caused its shining flank to get sheered off.

I lived in the dark, and didn't know at the time the awful blow I'd dealt him, only felt the panic blows he'd thrown at me.

**Alan Sillitoe,** *A Start in Life*

**Questions A**

1  How old do you think the storyteller was at the time this happened?  Why?
2  How long ago do you think this story took place?  Why?
3  Why was the man angry?
4  Why was the grandmother angry?
5  Whose fault was it that the car was damaged?  Why?
6  What is the meaning of the last sentence?

**Questions B**

Explain in your own words what the writer means by each of these phrases.

1  'a handful of . . . brazen curiosity'  (line 2)
2  'ominous bounces'  (line 18)
3  'the bewildered culprit'  (line 30)
4  'sent down'  (line 30)
5  'panic blows'  (line 39)

**Writing**

The man goes back into his house and tells his wife what has happened. Write their conversation.

*or*

The mother and grandmother take the child back into the house. Describe what happens and the conversation they have.

# She's leaving home

Wednesday morning at five o'clock as the day begins
Silently closing her bedroom door
Leaving a note that she hoped would say more
She goes downstairs to the kitchen clutching her handkerchief
Quietly turning the backdoor key
Stepping outside she is free.
    She          (We gave her most of our lives)
    is leaving    (Sacrificed most of our lives)
    home       (We gave her everything money could buy)
She's leaving home after living alone
For so many years. Bye, bye.

Father snores as his wife gets into her dressing gown
Picks up the letter that's lying there
Standing alone at the top of the stairs
She breaks down and cries to her husband
Daddy our baby's gone
Why should she treat us so thoughtlessly
How could she do this to me?
    She          (We never thought of ourselves)
    is leaving    (Never a thought of ourselves)
    home       (We struggled hard all our lives to get by)
She's leaving home after living alone
For so many years. Bye, bye.

Friday morning at nine o'clock she is far away
Waiting to keep an appointment she made
Meeting a man from the motor trade
    She          (What did we do that was wrong?)
    is leaving    (We didn't know it was wrong)
    home       (Fun is the one thing that money can't buy)
Something inside that was always denied
For so many years. Bye, bye.

**John Lennon** and **Paul McCartney**

# The Parents' Charter

A couple of kids stopped me in Oxford Street and sold me, for five pence, a smudgy copy of the Charter of Children's Rights.

They'd run it off on a duplicator in flagrant breach, I suspect, of the original copyright.

Anyway, full marks for initiative. And full marks, too, to the Children's Charter which – although this particular copy of it was practically indecipherable – I happen to know is full of good sense.

'Children have the right to privacy of person and thought . . . to freedom of expression . . . to freedom from political indoctrination . . .

'A child's personal appearance is his own and his family's concern . . . Children have the right to such knowledge as is necessary to understand the society in which they live . . . They shall have the freedom to make complaints about teachers and parents without fear of reprisal . . .'

Fine. Agreed. Accepted. Right on.

But, dear children, has it ever occurred to you that parents have their rights too? I would be very surprised if this revolutionary thought has ever entered your heads, and for that reason, I have drafted, for your consideration, a Charter of Parents' Rights.

Run it off on your duplicator by all means but don't try to sell it to me. Sell it to each other.

**Keith Waterhouse**

# *Jerusalem*

*Dave and Ada have moved from London to start a small carpentry business in the country. They are attempting to recapture the simple life and put socialist ideals into practice. Sammy works with Dave.*

SAMMY: It'll be a while before Ada comes, won't it?

DAVE: Yes.

SAMMY: I want a little word with you, then.

DAVE: Go on, son, I'm listening, but I must get this ready for glueing.

SAMMY: I want to leave soon.

DAVE: That was a very short word. Leave?

SAMMY: I aren't satisfied, Dave.

DAVE: Satisfied?

SAMMY: Well, I don't seem to be getting anywhere, then.

DAVE: But you're learning something, boy, you're learnin' to do something with your hands.

SAMMY: But nothing a factory can't do just as well as what we did.

DAVE: (*Shocked*) Have you ever seen inside a factory? You want to stand by a machine all day? By a planer or a sander or a saw bench?

SAMMY: They change around all the time.

DAVE: Excitement! You change machines! Big difference! All your life, Sammy, think of it, all your life.

SAMMY: But you get more money for it.

DAVE: That I do not have an answer to. (*Pause*) Sammy, remember that chair? Remember what you said about it? 'It looks as if it's sitting down,' you said. That's poetry, poetry. No, not poetry, what am I talking about? Look, er – it's – it's – O Jesus, how do you start explaining this thing? Look, Sammy, look at this rack you made for my chisels. Not an ordinary rack, not just bits of wood nailed together, but a special one with dove-tail joints and a mortice and tenon joint there, and look what you put on the side: remember you wanted to decorate it, so you used my carving tools and you worked out a design. For no reason at all you worked out a design on an ordinary chisel rack. But there was a reason really, wasn't there? You enjoyed using the tools and making up that design. I can remember watching you – a whole afternoon you spent on it and you used up three pieces of oak before you were satisfied. Twenty-seven and six you owe me.

SAMMY: Hell, that were only messing around.

DAVE: Not messing around. Creating! For the sheer enjoyment of it, just creating. And what about the fun we had putting up this workshop?

SAMMY:   It's not that I didn't enjoy myself, Dave.

DAVE:   But that's not all, cocker. It's not only the fun or the work – it's the place. Look at it, the place where we work. The sun reaches us, we get black in the summer. And any time we're fed up we pack up and go swimming. Don't you realise what that means? There's no one climbing on our backs. Free agents, Sammy boy; we enjoy our work, we like ourselves.

SAMMY:   You think I don't know these things? Hell, Dave. But I've seen the boys in the village, I know them. They don't care about things and I see them hang around all their lives, with twopence halfpenny between them and half a dozen dependants. But I want to get on – don't you think I ought to get on?

DAVE:   A bait! A trap! Don't take any notice of that clap-trap for God's sake, boy. For every hundred that are lured only one makes it. One, only one. Factories? Offices? When you're in those, mate, you're there for good. Can't you see that?

(*No answer.*)

No, you can't, can you? Of course you can't. Jesus, I must be mad to imagine I could fight everyone.

**Arnold Wesker,** *I'm Talking about Jerusalem*

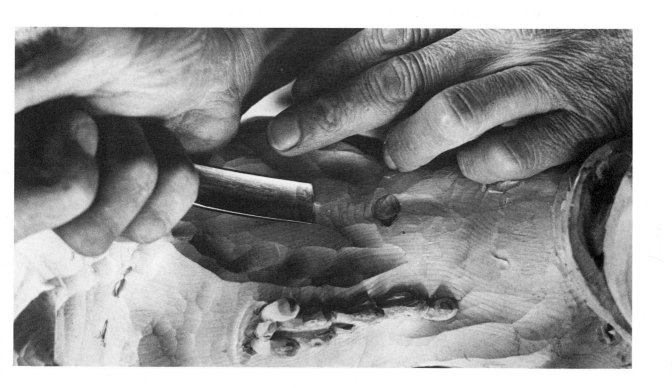

# The School Boy

I love to rise in a summer morn
When the birds sing on every tree;
The distant huntsman winds his horn,
And the sky-lark sings with me.
O! what sweet company.

But to go to school in a summer morn,
O! it drives all joy away;
Under a cruel eye outworn,
The little ones spend the day
In sighing and dismay.

Ah! then at times I drooping sit,
And spend many an anxious hour,
Nor in my book can I take delight,
Nor sit in learning's bower,
Worn through with the dreary shower.

How can the bird that is born for joy
Sit in a cage and sing?
How can a child, when fears annoy,
But droop his tender wing,
And forget his youthful spring?

O! father and mother, if buds are nipped
And blossoms blown away,
And if the tender plants are stripped
Of their joy in the springing day,
By sorrow and care's dismay,

How shall the summer arise in joy,
Or the summer fruits appear?
Or how shall we gather what griefs destroy,
Or bless the mellowing year,
When the blasts of winter appear?

**William Blake**

# *Schoolmaster*

The window gives onto the white trees.
The master looks out of it at the trees,
for a long time, he looks for a long time
out through the window at the trees,
breaking his chalk slowly in one hand.
And it's only the rules of long division.
And he's forgotten the rules of long division.
Imagine not remembering long division!
A mistake on the blackboard, a mistake.
We watch him with a different attention
needing no one to hint to us about it,
there's more than difference in this attention.
The schoolmaster's wife has gone away,
we do not know where she has gone to,
we do not know why she has gone,
what we know is his wife has gone away.

His clothes are neither new nor in the fashion;
wearing the suit which he always wears
and which is neither new nor in the fashion
the master goes downstairs to the cloakroom.
He fumbles in his pocket for a ticket.
'What's the matter? Where is that ticket?
Perhaps I never picked up my ticket.
Where is the thing?' Rubbing his forehead.
'Oh, here it is. I'm getting old.
Don't argue auntie dear, I'm getting old.
You can't do much about getting old.'
We hear the door below creaking behind him.

The window gives onto the white trees.
The trees there are high and wonderful,
but they are not why we are looking out.

We look in silence at the schoolmaster.
He has a bent back and clumsy walk,
he moves without defences, clumsily,
worn out I ought to have said, clumsily.
Snow falling on him softly through silence
turns him to white under the white trees.
He whitens into white like the trees.
A little longer will make him so white
we shall not see him in the whitened trees.

**Yevgeny Yevtushenko**

# Scenes from a bomber raid

## At base

Sweet smiled at the Group Captain to indicate how much he shared
his contempt for chairborne warriors. 'Especially when all a chap
wants to do is to get to grips with the damned Huns, sir.'

'That's it,' exclaimed the Groupie enthusiastically. 'I'm
employed to kill Huns, and by God, my squadron will kill more
Huns of all shapes, colours, sizes and sexes than any other in this
man's air force or I'll know the reason why.' The Groupie smiled
and self-deprecatingly added, 'At least, that's what I've told Air
Ministry a few times, eh?'

'Yes, sir,' said Sweet. 'In fact, on this matter of killing Huns
there's something you could help with . . . I say, I'm sorry to talk
shop and all that . . .'

'Now then,' said the Groupie. 'You know my views about
those bloody squadrons where they taboo shoptalk in the Mess.'

'Well, on this business of killing Huns, sir. There's a pilot – a
damn good chap, experienced, decorated and all that, a good NCO –
but he told me that he thinks our bombing attacks are "just old-
fashioned murder of working-class families".'

'Confounded fifth columnist!'

'Yes, sir, I knew you'd be annoyed, but that's not all. This war,
he says, is just the continuation of capitalism by other means.'

'That's Karl Marx he's quoting.'

'Yes. It's a misquote of Clausewitz actually, sir.'

'It's a bloody disgrace.'

## The first wave: over Altgarten

Altgarten now was a meaningless chaos of greens and yellows, fires,
photoflashes and explosions.

'The H2S is acting up, sir. I'm going to bomb the central fire,'
said Munro's bomb aimer.

'OK, bomb aimer,' said Munro. 'She's all yours.'

'Left, left, and a bit more. Now we're nice. Steady. Left, left.'

The fires were like little furry animals, their edges softened by
the smoke. And like animals they seemed to breathe, expanding and
contracting as the flames inhaled the surrounding air-currents.
Sometimes it was possible to see the tiny flicker of dozens of

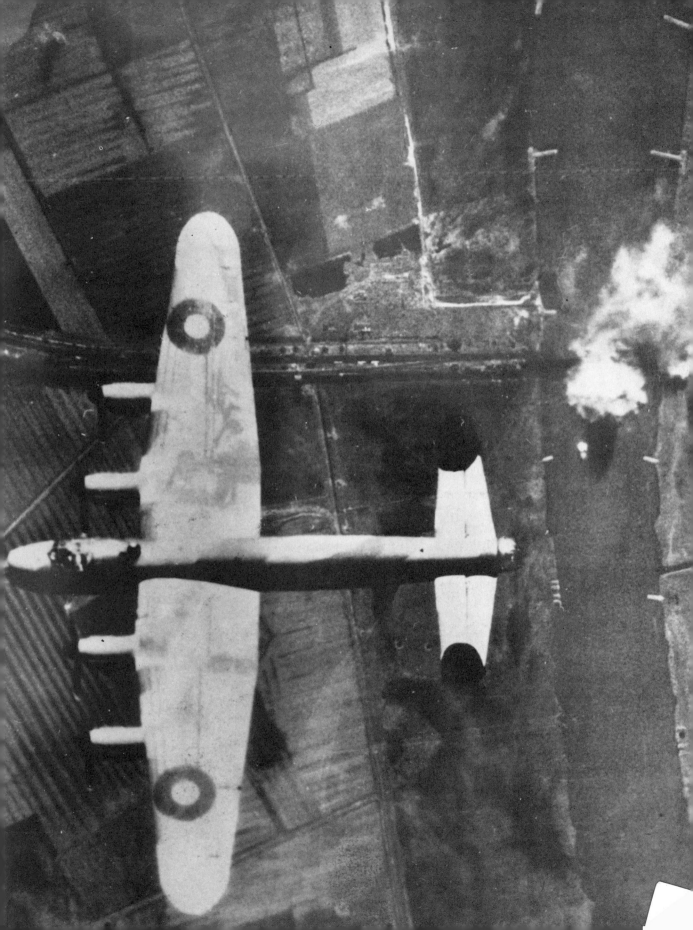

incendiaries as they landed and glowed pink. Much larger, the HE bombs flashed and were gone. From each aircraft came a photoflash bomb which exploded above the target with seven million candlepower of light that lasted longer than the bombs and threw enough light upwards to illuminate the bombers. One of these was going off every three or four seconds. Munro, listening carefully to his bomb aimer's instructions, saw by the light of one photoflash eight aeroplanes close around him and was so frightened that he made himself stare at his instrument panel.

'Left, left, steady.' There was no mistaking the instructions since the word 'left' was always said twice. Adding 'steady' without pausing was his way of telling Munro to only touch the left rudder. 'Steady, steady.' Plenty of flak now; the row of tiny fires crept along the bombsight wire with agonizing slowness. The Volkschule fire, the gasworks fire, the Nehringstrasse fire, the Altmarkt fire pulsated like red embers on a sooty fireplace. The bomb aimer waited for the largest one – the hospital annex – left, left, steady. The wire crossed the edge of it. 'Bombs gone.' The selector was at salvo. The whole bombload dropped away so that the Lancaster leapt into the air. Munro let the nose come up. For thirty seconds more they flew on straight and level, waiting for the photoflash to explode and the F24 camera shutter to turn over to record the accuracy of their bombing.

'OK.' Munro turned gently. 'Let's go home.'

Only a hundred yards behind him Jammy Giles was doing his best to follow his bomb aimer's instructions but he consistently overcorrected.

'Left, left,' said Alun. 'Right. Too far, left, left. Steady. No, too late. Right. Steady. Yes, that's good. Hold her like that. Steady. Left, left. Jammy, left, left, more.' The plane yawed across the target. The yellow markers slid past, well to the left of his bombsight mark. Under him came the Liebefrau church. The control column kicked against Jammy's sweaty grasp.

'Bombs gone, Jammy. Jettison bars across. It wasn't awfully good, I'm afraid.'

'Let's get out of here,' said Jammy.

# In the town

In the Rathaus the Burgomaster's telephones were ringing continually: '01.39. Florastrasse. High explosive. Fifteen wounded, two dead. Mains intact. Road blocked.'

The telephonist bit her lip as she impaled her written message upon the spike with the others. She lived in Florastrasse.

'01.40. Railway line near brewery. High explosive. No casualties. Railway blocked.'

'01.41. St Antonius Hospital. High explosive. Unknown casualties. Mains intact. Road blocked.'

Munro's cookie hit the St Antonius Hospital. It landed squarely upon the front steps of its neo-classical façade. The fine columns and the great pediment collapsed and some of the girders followed it. Luckily the front of the hospital consisted of offices, the main staircase, the lift, the inquiry desk and storerooms. One of the operating theatres was severely damaged too, although the boiler house below ground escaped. The heating system and hot-water supply were in full working order as soon as the broken pipes had been cut out of the system by screwing up the valves. The doorman lost one of his legs and a doctor suffered bad scalds on his upper body from the broken central heating. Two theatre nurses had to be treated for shock and small multiple injuries. Four patients were cut by flying glass. At the time it seemed a miracle that so little damage had been done to the hospital by such an enormous bomb.

On the other hand the raid had scarcely started yet and the damage to the steelwork had made the whole structure unsafe. More immediately, since the sloping ramps and the big – bedsize – lift shaft had gone, it meant that there was no way of evacuating the bedridden patients from the upper floors. In the wards the flashes of bombs and guns were lighting up the frightened faces of the trapped patients. The markers painted the sheets bright green and yellow and the shadows moved eerily across the floor and up the walls as the flares floated down upon the town. Everyone wanted attention: bed-pans, sleeping tablets, a drink of water or just a word of comfort. The ones that could walk insisted upon going to the toilet even though that was forbidden once the night shift began. They huddled at the window, these frightened, privileged, mobile few. One of the A Flight Lancs dropped a salvo near the Liebefrau church. Then Jammy Giles came across the town. 'Bombs gone, Jammy. It wasn't awfully good, I'm afraid.' The explosion shattered more of the hospital windows and threw a dozen patients full-length to the floor. The far end of Dorfstrasse was just hot rubble.

## The second wave hits Altgarten

When the second wave of bombers began their attack, both Gerd Böll and his friend Bodo Reuter knew that it was going to be even bigger than the first wave. This was the way the *Tommis* worked and the fast-revving British engines were as loud as a swarm of hornets. Salvoes of bombs were centring on the fires. The noise hammered their eardrums and the blast plucked at their bodies. They both knew that a sensible man would take cover, but they moved up Mönchenstrasse towards the hospital fire in leaps and runs punctuated by long waits flat on their faces.

Since Bodo's NCO had last visited the top floor, the roof had collapsed on one room, killing four radiographers. The floor tilted more now and there were cracks in the wall large enough to see through. Every minute or two the whole building groaned like an old man who has sat too long in one position, and like an old man it leaned a little more to one side. Always to the same side.

'Stay close to this wall,' Reuter ordered his men.

The floor lurched under them. The walls were bulging as the bricks expanded. The metal girders expanded too; pressed against the ceiling, writhing in the heat, they fired hot rivets across the room like bullets.

'How fast are they getting these people down?' asked Bodo.

'One team down the staircase, one by the airshaft. They are each taking about seven minutes.'

'Get the nurses out of here,' said Bodo.

'And the patients?'

'Get the nurses out.'

His Hauptwachmeister gave a perfunctory salute and turned to bellow at the men. 'You heard what the Oberzugführer said, evacuate all nurses to ground level. We will start on this floor.' Without delay the TENOs hurried after the NCO, rounding up the nursing staff and ordering them to leave their patients. The nurses began to argue, but orders are orders.

'How long do you think, Bodo?'

'Not more than ten minutes, Gerd.'

Neither Bodo nor Gerd saw the first row of beds go. One of the TENO messengers swore and a nurse screamed and then the far end of the ward was empty. The light of the fire lit the ceiling, for there was no longer any wall, it had exploded out into the courtyard along with the beds and people. The second row of beds screeched as they slid across the tilted lino, for the wheels had the safety brakes on, but gravity was too much for that device. The beds collided and interlocked. Thrashing blanketed bundles grabbed at pillars and lost their fingernails. A nurse overbalanced and she toppled over. She slid on her bottom across the highly polished floor, trying to hold her flying skirts down all the way until she fell off the edge and into the courtyard two storeys below.

They were screaming now. Hysterical screaming which neither alerts nor implores. Fatalistic yells and high-pitched cries were the final denunciation of an unjust world.

**Len Deighton,** *Bomber* (adapted)

INDIVIDUAL WORK

# *The brewery site*

Near the centre of the large town of Winterham is the brewery site. Originally there was a thriving brewery here, but thirty years ago it was closed down. The council bought the site and pulled down most of the buildings, except for the Old Brewery House, which dates from the 18th century. They planned to turn the site into a public park and recreation ground, but the only action they took was to put up swings, a roundabout and a slide, about twenty years ago. Now they want to sell the site to a supermarket chain and make a handsome profit. Not everyone agrees, however.

**Council view**

The play area is too close to busy main roads. There have already been several accidents, some quite serious. When the site is sold, a new play area will be set up on the outskirts of the town, with much better facilities.

**Opponents' view**

Children have played here for twenty years without many accidents. Those there were could have been avoided if the council had put up a proper fence. If the site is sold, there will be nowhere near the centre of town for children to play.

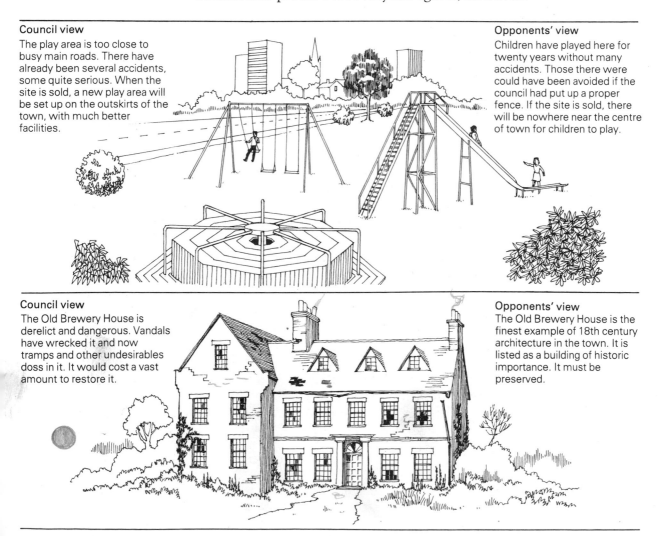

**Council view**

The Old Brewery House is derelict and dangerous. Vandals have wrecked it and now tramps and other undesirables doss in it. It would cost a vast amount to restore it.

**Opponents' view**

The Old Brewery House is the finest example of 18th century architecture in the town. It is listed as a building of historic importance. It must be preserved.

**Council view**

The rest of the site is overgrown and ugly. The so-called 'pond' is a stretch of stagnant water that smells in summer and is a hazard to health.

**Opponents' view**

The site has gradually developed into a miniature nature reserve in the centre of a large town. The pond provides a habitat for many interesting and unusual plants and animals. The site is one of the few remaining breedings grounds for the 'Lancashire Little Mauve' moth.

**Writing**

Study both sides of the argument carefully. Think of further points that each side could make, and do not feel limited by the pictures and words that are given. Then present both sides of the argument in one of the following forms.

1   An exchange of letters in the local newspaper. Possible correspondents: local councillors, the chairman of the Brewery Site Protection Group, the manager of the supermarket chain.

2   A series of interviews between an investigating reporter from the local radio station and people involved.

**Research**

Choose a topic about which people have strong opinions. It may be a local or a national issue. Make a list of questions to ask people related to the topic. Decide who you are going to interview. As you interview them make notes of their answers. When you have finished the series of interviews, write a report on your findings.

**Story writing**

1   Write a story that includes one of these snippets of conversation.
'I don't agree with it at all.'
'Why not?'
'It's wrong, that's why. And I'm surprised you have to ask!'

'I never did like her.'
'Nor me.'
'I never agreed with anything she said.'
'Me neither.'

2   Think of a story that has at least two important characters in it. Write two versions of the story: one as the first character sees it; and one as told by the second character.

# Rites and Ceremonies

1

2

How many of these
ceremonies can you
identify?

3

4  5

# Meeting Kondén Diara

*In many countries there are special rituals that young people have to go through before they are accepted as adults. Camara Laye grew up in a small village in Guinea, West Africa. As a young boy he had to go through the ordeal of 'meeting Kondén Diara'.*

Now I was not unaware who Kondén Diara was: my mother had threatened me only too often with that terrible bogeyman, that 'lion that eats up little boys'. Was he a man? Was he an animal? Was he not rather half-man, half-animal?

As soon as our elders had made sure that no intruder was present, we left the town behind and entered the bush by a path which leads to a sacred place where each year the initiation takes place. It is situated under an enormous bombax tree, a hollow at the junction of the River Komoni and the River Niger.

Just before we reached the hollow we saw flames leap up from a huge wood fire that the bushes had hidden from us until then. I quickened my steps – we all quickened our steps – and the crimson radiance of the fire enveloped us. We assembled beneath the bombax tree. The ground beneath had been cleared of reeds and tall grasses.

Our elders suddenly shouted, 'Kneel!'

We at once fell to our knees.

'Heads down!'

We lowered our heads.

'Lower than that!'

We bent our heads right to the ground, as if in prayer.

'Now hide your eyes!'

We don't have to be told twice; we shut our eyes tight and press our hands over them. For would we not die of fright and horror if we should see, or so much as catch a glimpse of Kondén Diara? Our elders walk up and down behind us and in front of us, to make sure that we had all obeyed their orders. Now that we are on our knees with our foreheads to the ground and our hands pressed over our eyes, Kondén Diara's roaring suddenly bursts out.

We were expecting to hear this hoarse roar, we were not expecting any other sound, but it takes us by surprise, and shatters us, freezes our hearts with its unexpectedness. And it is not only a lion, it is not only Kondén Diara roaring: there are ten, twenty, perhaps thirty lions that take their lead from him, uttering their terrible roars and surrounding the hollow; ten or thirty lions separated from us by a few yards only and that the great wood fire will perhaps not always keep at bay; No, not one of us would dream of venturing to open an eye, not one! Not one of us would dare to lift his head from the ground, he would rather bury it in the earth. And I bend down as far as I can: we all bend down farther, we bend our knees as much as we can, we keep our backs as low as possible; I make myself, we all make ourselves as small as we can.

Not for a single instant do I doubt the presence of the monster. Who could assemble such a numerous herd, if not Kondén Diara? 'He alone,' I said to myself, 'he alone has such power over lions . . . Keep away, Kondén Diara! Keep away! Go back into the bush! . . .' But Kondén Diara went on with his revels, and sometimes it seemed to me that he roared right over my own head, right in my own ears even. 'Keep away, I implore thee, Kondén Diara!'

What was it my father had said? 'Kondén Diara roars; but he won't do more than roar; he will not take you away . . .' Yes, something like that. But is it true, really true? There is also a rumour that Kondén Diara sometimes pounces with fearsome claws on someone or other and carries him far away, far, far away into the depths of the bush; and then, days and days afterwards, months or even years later, quite by chance a huntsman may discover some whitened bones . . . And do not people also die of fright? . . . Ah! how I wish this roaring would stop! How I wish . . . How I wish I was far away from this clearing, back in the compound, in the warm security of the hut! . . . Will this roaring never end? . . . 'Go away Kondén Diara! Go away! . . . Stop roaring . . .' Oh! those roars! . . . I feel as if I can bear them no longer . . .

Whereupon, suddenly, they stop! They stop just as they had begun. Is it over? Really over? . . . Is it not just a temporary interruption? . . . No, I dare not feel relieved just yet. And then suddenly the voice of one of the older boys rings out:

'Get up!'

I heave a sigh of relief. This time, it's really over. We look at one another: I look at Kouyaté and the others. If there was only a little more light . . . But the light from the fire is sufficient: great drops of sweat are still beading our foreheads; yet the night is chill . . . Yes, we were afraid. We were not able to conceal our fear . . .

**Camara Laye,** *The African Child*

|  |  |
|---|---|
| Questions to think and talk about | 1 What do you think is the purpose of this ritual? |
|  | 2 What do you imagine the boys actually heard? |
|  | 3 Are there any initiation rites in this country? |
|  | 4 If so, what are they? |
|  | 5 If not, why do you think this is? |
| Writing | 1 This story describes a moment of great fear in a person's life. Write an account of what it is like to be really frightened. It may be a poem or a story. It may describe a real event or an imaginary one. |
|  | 2 Write a story or a poem entitled 'The dare'. |

# Initiation among the Amazon Indians

### The Carib girl's ceremony

When a Carib girl is about 14 years old, her mother builds her a small hut of palm leaves within the family house. The girl must remain inside this hut for eight days, without talking to anyone and just spinning cotton.

At the end of eight days, the girl's mother invites to the house an elderly couple who are known to be hard workers. The girl comes out of her hut and the old woman places some cotton in her hands and sets light to it. In order not to get scorched, the girl quickly throws the cotton from hand to hand until it is all burnt up. Then the old man takes the girl's hands and puts them for a moment in a small bowl filled with large, biting ants.

The purpose of these stages in the ceremony is to remind the girl that she should be a hard worker. When handling cotton, her hands should always move quickly just as they did when she tossed

the burning cotton from hand to hand during the ceremony. In all other aspects of life she should also work hard, just as the ants in the bowl are thought to.

Finally, the girl is dressed up in a loincloth, necklaces, bracelets and earrings, and her body is painted. Other visitors are served manioc beer and dance and sing while the girl watches from her hammock.

### The Panare boy's ceremony

Panare boys go through an initiation ceremony when they are between 8 and 12 years old. The most important part of this ceremony is the dressing of each boy for the first time in a loincloth, with bead armbands and other decorations that symbolize that he is about to become an adult. The ceremony is carried out in stages during three large, public dances, held during the dry season. Each dance lasts for twenty-four hours, from nightfall until nightfall, but there are breaks of several weeks between them.

During the dances, the initiation ceremony is mixed with the celebration of hunting, fishing and crop growing. Most of the songs sung during the first two dances are about the animals and fish that the Panare eat. For much of the time, the boys have to stand completely still at the edge of the dancing area.

In the third dance, however, the initiation of the boys becomes the centre of attention. The day before the dance, the boys are taken into the forest where they are given special medicines to make them strong. The songs in the third dance are about the things that the boys will wear for the first time. The following afternoon, the boys' are dressed by men who have been specially invited from other villages. Afterwards everyone, except the boys, joins together in a huge feast of smoked meat and manioc bread.

The next day, the newly initiated boys go out into the forest alone for the first time. But although they now dress like adults, they will not be considered grown-up until they have learnt how to hunt, fish and make clearings in the forest.

**Paul Henley,** *Amazon Indians*

Questions
1 What is the first part of the Carib girl's ceremony?
2 Why does she have to handle the burning cotton?
3 How are ants used in the ceremony?
4 What is the purpose of this?
5 How do the visitors celebrate her initiation?
6 At what time of year are Panare boys initiated?
7 How many main stages are there to this initiation?
8 What do the boys do before the third dance?
9 What do they sing about during the third dance?
10 What else do they have to do before they are considered grown-up?

# Church wedding

## 1662

*Then shall the Minister say,*

Who giveth this woman to be married to this man?

*Then shall they give their troth to each other in this manner.*
*The Minister, receiving the Woman at her father's or friend's hands, shall cause the Man with his right hand to take the Woman by her right hand, and to say after him as followeth.*

I N. take thee *N.* to my wedded wife, to have and to hold from this day forward, for better for worse, for richer for poorer, in sickness and in health, to love and to cherish, till death us do part, according to God's holy ordinance; and thereto I plight thee my troth.

*Then shall they loose their hands; and the Woman, with her right hand taking the Man by his right hand, shall likewise say after the Minister,*

I N. take thee N. to my wedded husband, to have and to hold from this day forward, for better for worse, for richer for poorer, in sickness and in health, to love, cherish, and to obey, till death us do part, according to God's holy ordinance; and thereto I give thee my troth.

*Then shall they again loose their hands; and the Man shall give unto the Woman a Ring, laying the same upon the book with the accustomed duty to the Priest and Clerk. And the Priest, taking the Ring, shall deliver it unto the Man, to put it upon the fourth finger of the Woman's left hand. And the Man holding the Ring there, and taught by the Priest, shall say,*

W ITH this ring I thee wed, with my body I thee worship, and with all my worldly goods I thee endow: In the Name of the Father, and of the Son, and of the Holy Ghost. Amen.

*Then the Man leaving the Ring upon the fourth finger of the Woman's left hand, they shall both kneel down, and the Minister shall say,*

Let us pray.

*Book of Common Prayer 1662*

Wedding about 1820

# 1980

The priest may receive the bride from the hands of her father.
The bride and bridegroom face each other.
The bridegroom takes the bride's right hand in his, and says

> I, N, take you, N,
> to be my wife,
> to have and to hold
> from this day forward;
> for better, for worse,
> for richer, for poorer,
> in sickness and in health,
> to love and to cherish,
> till death us do part,
> according to God's holy law;
> and this is my solemn vow.

They loose hands.
The bride takes the bridegroom's right hand in hers, and says

> I, N, take you, N,
> to be my husband,
> to have and to hold
> from this day forward,
> for better, for worse,
> for richer, for poorer,
> in sickness and in health,
> to love and to cherish,
> till death us do part,

> according to God's holy law;
> and this is my solemn vow.

They loose hands.
The priest receives the ring(s). He says

> Heavenly Father, by your blessing, let this ring be to N and N a symbol of unending love and faithfulness, to remind them of the vow and convenant which they have made this day; through Jesus Christ our Lord. Amen.

The bridegroom places the ring on the fourth finger of the bride's left hand, and holding it there, says,

> I give you this ring as a sign of our marriage. With my body I honour you, all that I am I give to you, and all that I have I share with you, within the love of God, Father, Son, and Holy Spirit.

If only one ring is used, before they loose hands, the bride says,

> I receive this ring as a sign of our marriage. With my body I honour you, all that I am I give to you, and all that I have I share with you, within the love of God, Father, Son, and Holy Spirit.

*Alternative Service Book* 1980

Wedding 1980

# 'Blackie, The Electric Rembrandt'

We watch through the shop-front while
Blackie draws stars – an equal

concentration on his and
the youngster's faces. The hand

is steady and accurate;
but the boy does not see it

for his eyes follow the point
that touches (quick, dark movement!)

a virginal arm beneath
his rolled sleeve: he holds his breath.

. . . Now that it is finished, he
hands a few bills to Blackie

and leaves with a bandage on
his arm, under which gleam ten

stars, hanging in a blue thick
cluster. Now he is starlike.

**Thom Gunn**

# Gunpowder Plot

For days these curious cardboard buds have lain
In brightly coloured boxes. Soon the night
Will come. We pray there'll be no sullen rain
To make these magic orchids flame less bright.

Now in the garden's darkness they begin
To flower: the frenzied whizz of Catherine-wheel
Puts forth its fiery petals and the thin
Rocket soars to burst upon the steel

Bulwark of a cloud. And then the guy,
Absurdly human phoenix, is again
Gulped by greedy flames: the harvest sky
Is flecked with threshed and glittering golden grain.

'Uncle! A cannon! Watch me as I light it!'
The women helter-skelter, squealing high,
Retreat; the paper fuse is quickly lit,
A cat-like hiss, and spit of fire, a sly

Falter, then the air is shocked with blast.
The cannon bangs and in my nostrils drifts
A bitter scent that brings the lurking past
Lurching to my side. The present shifts,

Allows a ten-year memory to walk
Unhindered now; and so I'm forced to hear
The banshee howl of mortar and the talk
Of men who died, am forced to taste my fear.

I listen for a moment to the guns,
The torn earth's grunts, recalling how I prayed.
The past retreats. I hear a corpse's sons –
'Who's scared of bangers!' 'Uncle! John's afraid!'

**Vernon Scannell**

# The Law of Life

Old Koskoosh listened greedily. Though his sight had long since faded, his hearing was still acute, and the slightest sound penetrated to the glimmering intelligence which yet abode behind the withered forehead, but which no longer gazed forth upon the things of the world. Ah! That was Sit-cum-to-ha, shrilly anathematizing the dogs as she cuffed and beat them into the harnesses. Sit-cum-to-ha was his daughter's daughter, but she was too busy to waste a thought upon her broken grandfather, sitting alone there in the snow, forlorn and helpless. Camp must be broken. The long trail waited while the short day refused to linger. Life called her, and the duties of life, not death. And he was very close to death now.

The thought made the old man panicky for the moment, and he stretched forth a palsied hand which wandered tremblingly over the small heap of dry wood beside him. Reassured that it was indeed there, his hand returned to the shelter of his mangy furs, and he again fell to listening. The sulky crackling of half-frozen hides told him that the chief's moose-skin lodge had been struck, and even then was being rammed and jammed into portable compass. The chief was his son, stalwart and strong, headman of the tribesmen, and a mighty hunter. As the women toiled with the camp luggage, his voice rose, chiding them for their slowness. Old Koskoosh strained his ears. It was the last time he would hear that voice. There went Geehow's lodge! And Tusken's! Seven, eight, nine; only the shaman's could be still standing. There! They were at work upon it now. He could hear the shaman grunt as he piled it on the sled. A child whimpered, and a woman soothed it with soft, crooning gutturals. Little Kootee, the old man thought, a fretful child, and not overstrong. It would die soon, perhaps, and they would burn a hole through the frozen tundra and pile rocks above to keep the wolverines away. Well, what did it matter? A few years at best, and as many an empty belly as a full one. And in the end, Death waited, ever-hungry and hungriest of them all.

What was that? Oh, the men lashing the sleds and drawing tight the thongs. He listened, who would listen no more. The whiplashes snarled and bit among the dogs. Hear them whine! How they hated the work and the trail! They were off! Sled after sled churned slowly away into the silence. They were gone. They had passed out of his life, and he faced the last bitter hour alone. No. The snow crunched beneath a moccasin; a man stood beside him; upon his head a hand rested gently. His son was good to do this thing. He remembered other old men whose sons had not waited after the tribe. But his son had. He wandered away into the past, till the young man's voice brought him back.

'It is well with you?' he asked.

And the old man answered, 'It is well.'

'There be wood beside you,' the younger man continued, 'and the fire burns bright. The morning is gray, and the cold has broken. It will snow presently. Even now it is snowing.'

'Aye, even now is it snowing.'

'The tribesmen hurry. Their bales are heavy and their bellies flat with lack of feasting. The trail is long and they travel fast. I go now. It is well?'

'It is well. I am a last year's leaf, clinging lightly to the stem. The first breath that blows, and I fall. My voice is become like an old woman's. My eyes no longer show me the way of my feet, and my feet are heavy, and I am tired. It is well.'

He bowed his head in content till the last noise of the complaining snow had died away, and he knew his son was beyond

recall. Then his hand crept out in haste to the wood. It alone stood between him and the eternity that yawned in upon him. At last the measure of his life was a handful of faggots. One by one they would go to feed the fire, and just so, step by step, death would creep upon him. When the last stick had surrendered up its heat, the frost would begin to gather strength. First his feet would yield, then his hands; and the numbness would travel, slowly, from the extremities to the body. His head would fall forward upon his knees, and he would rest. It was easy. All men must die.

He did not complain. It was the way of life, and it was just. He had been born close to the earth. It was the law of all flesh. Nature was not kindly to the flesh. She had no concern for that concrete thing called the individual. Her interest lay in the species, the race. This was the deepest abstraction old Koskoosh's barbaric mind was capable of, but he grasped it firmly. He saw it exemplified in all life. The rise of the sap, the bursting greenness of the willow bud, the fall of the yellow leaf – in this alone was told the whole history. But one task did Nature set the individual. Did he not perform it, he died. Did he perform it, it was all the same, he died. Nature did not care; there were plenty who were obedient, and it was only the obedience in this matter, not the obedient, which lived and lived always. The tribe of Koskoosh was very old. The old men he had known when a boy had known old men before them. Therefore it was true that the tribe lived, that it stood for the obedience of all its members, way down into the forgotten past, whose very resting places were unremembered. They did not count; they were episodes. They had passed away like clouds from a summer sky. He also was an episode and would pass away. Nature did not care. To life she set one task, gave one law. To perpetuate was the task of life, its law was death. A maiden was a good creature to look upon, full-breasted and strong, with spring to her step and light in her eyes. But her task was yet before her. The light in her eyes brightened, her step quickened, she was now bold with the young men, now timid, and she gave them of her own unrest. And ever she grew fairer and yet fairer to look upon, till some hunter, able no longer to withhold himself, took her to his lodge to cook and toil for him and to become the mother of his children. And with the coming of her offspring her looks left her. Her limbs dragged and shuffled, her eyes dimmed and bleared, and only the little children found joy against the withered cheek of the old squaw by the fire. Her task was done. But a little while, on the first pinch of famine or the first long trail, and she would be left, even as he had been left, in the snow, with a little pile of wood. Such was the law.

**Jack London,** *The Law of Life*

# *New every morning*

'Hymn number one-seven-five, "New every morning is the love".'

The navy blue covers of the hymn books, inconspicuous against the boys' clothing, bloomed white across the hall as they were opened and the pages flicked through. The scuff and tick of the turning pages was slowly drowned under a rising chorus of coughing until Mr Gryce, furious behind the lectern, scooped up his stick and began to smack it vertically down the face.

'STOP THAT INFERNAL COUGHING'.

The sight and swishsmack of the stick stopped the throat noises and the boys and the teachers, posted at regular intervals at the ends of the rows, all looked up at the platform. Gryce was straining over the top of the lectern like a bulldog upon its hind legs.

'It's every morning alike! As soon as the hymn is announced you're off revving up! Hm-hmmm! Hm-hmm! It's more like a race track in here than an assembly hall!'

Not a foot scraped. Not a page stirred. The teachers looked seriously into the ranks of boys. The boys stood looking up at Gryce, each one convinced that Gryce was looking at him.

The silence thickened; the boys began to swallow their Adam's apples, their eyes skittering about in still heads. The teachers began to glance at each other and glance sideways up at the platform.

Then a boy coughed.

'Who did that?'

Everybody looking round.

'I said WHO DID THAT?'

The teachers moved in closer, alert like a riot squad.

'Mr Crossley! Somewhere near you! Didn't you see the boy?'

Crossley flushed, and rushed amongst them, thrusting them aside in panic.

'There, Crossley! That's where it came from! Around there!'

Crossley grabbed a boy and began to yank him into the open.

'It wasn't me, Sir!'

'Of course it was you.'

'It wasn't, Sir, honest!'

Gryce thrust his jaw over the front of the lectern, the air whistling down his nostrils.

'MACDOWALL! I might have known it! Get to my room, lad!'

Crossley escorted MacDowall from the hall. Gryce waited for the doors to stop swinging, then replaced his stick and addressed the school.

'Right. We'll try again. Hymn one hundred and seventy-five.'

The pianist struck the chord. Moderately slow it said in the book, but this direction was ignored by the school, and the tempo they produced was dead slow, the words delivered in a grinding monotone.

'New ev-ery morn-ing is the love
Our waken-ing and up-ris-ing prove;
Through sleep and dark-ness safe-ly brought,
Re-stored to life, and power, and thought.'

'STOP.'

The pianist stopped playing. The boys stopped singing.

'And what's that noise supposed to represent? I've heard sweeter sounds in a slaughter house! This is supposed to be a hymn of joy, not a dirge! So get your heads up, and your books up, and open your mouths, and SING.'

There was a mass bracing of backs and showing of faces as Gryce stepped round the lectern to the edge of the platform and leaned out over the well of the hall.

'Or I'll make you sing like you've never sung before.'

The words came out in a whisper, but they were as audible to the older boys at the back of the hall as to the small boys staring up under his chin.

'Verse two – New mercies each returning day.'

Gryce retreated, and the remaining four verses were completed without interruption, verse two with increased volume, deteriorating through three and four, to the concluding verse, which was delivered in the original monotone.

Before all the hymn books had been closed, and with the last notes still in the air, a boy came forward from the drapes at the back of the platform, and while still in motion began to read from the Bible held close to his chest.

'Thismorning'sreadingistakenfromMattheweighteen-verses . . .'

'Louder, boy. And stop mumbling into your beard.'

'Never despise one of these little ones I tell you they have their guardian angels in heaven who look continually on the face of my heavenly Father. What do you think suppose a man has a hundred sheep if one of them strays does he not leave the other ninety-nine on the hillside and go in search of the one that strayed. And if he should find it I tell you this he is more delighted over that sheep than over the ninety-nine that never strayed. In the same way it is your heavenly Father's will that one of these little ones should be lost here ends this morning's reading.'

He closed the Bible and backed away, his relief pathetic to see.

'We will now sing the Lord's Prayer. Eyes closed. Heads bowed.'

**Barry Hines,** *Kes*

# A calendar of festivals

| | | |
|---|---|---|
| January | 1 | New Year's Day |
| | 6 | Epiphany |
| February | 14 | St Valentine's Day |
| | | Meelad al Nabi: Birth of the Prophet Mohammed |
| February/March | .................... | |
| | | Ash Wednesday |
| March | 1 | St David's Day |
| | 17 | St Patrick's Day |
| | | Holi |
| March/April | .................... | |
| | | Good Friday |
| | | Easter Day |
| April | 23 | .................... |
| May | 1 | May Day |
| | | Vesakha |
| May/June | | Shovous |
| | | Whit Sunday |
| July/August | | Rakshabandhan |
| September/October | | Rish Hashanah/Yom Kippur |
| October | 31 | Hallowe'en |
| October/November | | .................... |
| November | 5 | Guy Fawkes' Day |
| | 30 | St Andrew's Day |
| December | 25 | Christmas Day |
| | 26 | Boxing Day/St Stephen's Day |

**Writing**
1 Copy out the table.
2 Fit these four festivals into the blanks:
   Shrove Tuesday    St George's Day
   Pesach (Passover)    Diwali
3 Add any other festivals and public holidays that you know about.

**Research**
1 Find out *who* celebrates each of the following and *what* is celebrated.
   Epiphany    Holi    Vesakha
   Shovous    Whit Sunday

# Jumbled story

The following passage is about the Aboriginal initiation rite known as a walkabout. It has been divided into seven sections, which have been printed in the wrong order. Study them carefully and decide what should be the correct order. Then write down the numbers in that order.

1   The test consisted of journeying from one group of waterholes to another; a journey which invariably took some six to eight months and was made entirely unaided and alone.

2   There was a time to be weaned, a time to be carried in arms: a time to walk with the tribe, a time to walk alone: a time for the proving-of-manhood, a time for the taking of gins (wives).

3   In the bush boy's tribe, every male who reached the age of thirteen or fourteen had to perform a walkabout – a selective test which weeded out and exterminated the weaker members of the tribe, and ensured that only the fittest survived to father children.

4   To the bush boy everything had its appointed time.

5   This custom is not common to all Aboriginal tribes, but is confined to the Bindaboo, the most primitive and least-known of the Aboriginal groups, who live among the water-holes of the Central and North Australian desert.

6   A boy couldn't walk before he'd been weaned; couldn't take a gin before his manhood had been proved. These things were done in order.

7   A time for hunting and a time to die. These times were pre-ordained. They never overlapped.

**James Vance Marshall,** *Walkabout*

# Ted Hughes

A poet talks about poetry

Ted Hughes was born in 1930. He has written poetry, plays, and stories. Some of his poetry is written for adults and some especially for young people. He has also spent a lot of time encouraging people at school to write their own poetry and advising them on ways in which to approach writing. In this unit we look at some of the things he has said about writing poetry and also at some of his own poems. There are suggestions about ways in which you can write your own poems.

Among the books that Ted Hughes has written especially for young people are:

*The Earth-Owl and Other Moon People*
*Meet My Folks!*
*How the Whale Became*
*The Iron Man*
*Nessie the Mannerless Monster*
*Season Songs*
*Under the North Star*
(all published by Faber and Faber Ltd.)

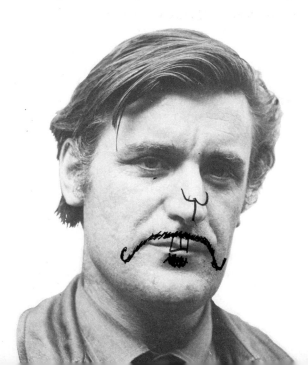

# *Capturing animals*

There are all sorts of ways of capturing animals and birds and fish. I spent most of my time, up to the age of fifteen or so, trying out many of these ways and when my enthusiasm began to wane, as it did gradually, I started to write poems.

You might not think that these two interests, capturing animals and writing poems, have much in common. But the more I think back the more sure I am that with me the two interests have been one interest. My pursuit of mice at threshing time when I was a boy, snatching them from under the sheaves as the sheaves were lifted away out of the stack and popping them into my pocket till I had thirty or forty crawling around in the lining of my coat, that and my present pursuit of poems seem to me to be different stages of the same fever. In a way, I suppose, I think of poems as a sort of animal. They have their own life, like animals, by which I mean that they seem quite separate from any person, even from their author, and nothing can be added to them or taken away without maiming and perhaps even killing them. And they have a certain wisdom. They know something special . . . something perhaps which we are very curious to learn. Maybe my concern has been to capture not animals particularly and not poems, but simply things which have a vivid life of their own, outside mine. However all that may be, my interest in animals began when I began. My memory goes back pretty clearly to my third year, and by then I had so many of the toy lead animals you could buy in shops that they went right round our flat-topped fender, nose to tail, with some over.

I had a gift for modelling and drawing, so when I discovered plasticine my zoo became infinite, and when an aunt bought me a thick green-backed animal book for my fourth birthday I began to draw the glossy photographs. The animals looked good in the photographs, but they looked even better in my drawings and were mine. I can remember very vividly the excitement with which I used to sit staring at my drawings, and it is a similar thing I feel nowadays with poems.

My zoo was not entirely an indoors affair. At that time we lived in a valley in the Pennines in West Yorkshire. My brother, who probably had more to do with this passion of mine than anyone else, was a good bit older than I was, and his one interest in life was creeping about on the hillsides with a rifle. He took me along as a retriever and I had to scramble into all kinds of places collecting magpies and owls and rabbits and weasels and rats and curlews that he shot. He could not shoot enough for me. At the same time I used to be fishing daily in the canal, with the long-handled wire-rimmed curtain mesh sort of net.

All that was only the beginning. When I was about eight, we moved to an industrial town in south Yorkshire. Our cat went upstairs and moped in my bedroom for a week, it hated the place so much, and my brother for the same reason left home and became a gamekeeper. But in many ways that move of ours was the best thing that ever happened to me. I soon discovered a farm in the nearby country that supplied all my needs, and soon after, a private estate, with woods and lakes.

My friends were town boys, sons of colliers and railwaymen, and with them I led one life, but all the time I was leading this other life on my own in the country. I never mixed the two lives up, except once or twice disastrously. I still have some diaries that I kept in those years: they record nothing but my catches.

Finally, as I have said, at about fifteen my life grew more complicated and my attitude to animals changed. I accused myself of disturbing their lives. I began to look at them, you see, from their own point of view.

And about the same time I began to write poems. Not animal poems. It was years before I wrote what you could call an animal poem and several more years before it occurred to me that my writing poems might be partly a continuation of my earlier pursuit. Now I have no doubt. The special kind of excitement, the slightly mesmerized and quite involuntary concentration with which you make out the stirrings of a new poem in your mind, then the outline, the mass and colour and clean final form of it, the unique living reality of it in the midst of the general lifelessness, all that is too familiar to mistake. This is hunting and the poem is a new species of creature, a new specimen of the life outside your own.

I have now told you very briefly what I believe to be the origins and growth of my interest in writing poetry. I have simplified everything a great deal, but on the whole that is the story. Some of it may seem a bit obscure to you. How can a poem, for instance, about a walk in the rain, be like an animal? Well, perhaps it cannot look much like a giraffe or an emu or an octupus, or anything you might find in an menagerie. It is better to call it an assembly of living parts moved by a single spirit. The living parts are the words, the images, the rhythms. The spirit is the life which inhabits them when they all work together. It is impossible to say which comes first, parts or spirit. But if any of the parts are dead . . . if any of the words, or images or rhythms do not jump to life as you read them . . . then the creature is going to be maimed and the spirit sickly. So, as a poet, you have to make sure that all those parts over which you have control, the words and rhythms and images, are alive. That is where the difficulties begin. Yet the rules, to begin with, are very simple. Words that live are those which we hear, like 'click' or 'chuckle', or which we see, like 'freckled' or 'veined', or which we taste, like 'vinegar' or 'sugar', or touch, like 'prickle' or 'oily', or smell, like 'tar' or 'onion'. Words which belong directly to one of the five senses. Or words which act and seem to use their muscles, like 'flick' or 'balance'.

But immediately things become more difficult. 'Click' not only gives you a sound, it gives you the motion of a sharp movement . . . such as your tongue makes in saying 'click'. It also gives you the feel of something light and brittle, like a snapping twig. Heavy things do not click, nor do soft bendable ones. In the same way, tar not only smells strongly. It is sticky to touch, with a particular thick and choking stickiness. Also it moves, when it is soft, like a black snake, and has a beautiful black gloss. So it is with most words. They belong to several of the senses at once, as if each one had eyes, ears and tongue, or ears and fingers and a body to move with. It is this little goblin in a word which is its life and its poetry, and it is this goblin which the poet has to have under control.

Well, you will say, this is hopeless. How do you control all that. When the words are pouring out how can you be sure that you do not have one of these side meanings of the word 'feathers' getting all stuck up with one of the side meanings of the word 'treacle', a few words later. In bad poetry this is exactly what happens, the words kill each other. Luckily, you do not have to bother about it so long as you do one thing.

That one thing is, imagine what you are writing about. See it and live it. Do not think it up laboriously, as if you were working out mental arithmetic. Just look at it, touch it, smell it, listen to it, turn yourself into it. When you do this, the words look after themselves, like magic. If you do this you do not have to bother about commas or full-stops or that sort of thing. You do not look at the words either. You keep your eyes, your ears, your nose, your taste, your touch, your whole being on the thing you are turning into words. The minute you flinch, and take your mind off this thing, and begin to look at the words and worry about them . . . then your worry goes into them and they set about killing each other. So you keep going as long as you can, then look back and see what you have written. After a bit of practice, and after telling yourself a few times that you do not care how other people have written about this thing, this is the way you find it; and after telling yourself you are going to use any old word that comes into your head so long as it seems right at the moment of writing it down, you will surprise yourself. You will read back through what you have written and you will get a shock. You will have captured a spirit, a creature.

After all that, I ought to give you some examples and show you some of my own more recently acquired specimens.

An animal I never succeeded in keeping alive is the fox. I was always frustrated: twice by a farmer, who killed cubs I had caught before I could get to them, and once by a poultry keeper who freed my cub while his dog waited. Years after those events I was sitting up late one snowy night in dreary lodgings in London. I had written nothing for a year or so but that night I got the idea I might write something and I wrote in a few minutes the following poem: the first 'animal' poem I ever wrote. Here it is—*The Thought-Fox*.

I imagine this midnight moment's forest:
Something else is alive
Beside the clock's loneliness
And this blank page where my fingers move,

Through the window I see no star:
Something more near
Though deeper within darkness
Is entering the loneliness:

Cold, delicately as the dark snow,
A fox's nose touches twig, leaf;
Two eyes serve a movement, that now
And again now, and now, and now

Sets neat prints into the snow
Between trees, and warily a lame
Shadow lags by stump and in hollow
Of a body that is bold to come

Across clearings, an eye,
A widening deepening greenness,
Brilliantly, concentratedly,
Coming about its own business

Till, with a sudden sharp hot stink of fox
It enters the dark hole of the head.
The window is starless still; the clock ticks,
The page is printed.

This poem does not have anything you could easily call a meaning. It is about a fox, obviously enough, but a fox that is both a fox and not a fox. What sort of a fox is it that can step right into my head where presumably it still sits . . . smiling to itself when the dogs bark. It is both a fox and a spirit. It is a real fox; as I read the poem I see it move, I see it setting its prints, I see its shadow going over the irregular surface of the snow. The words show me all this, bringing it nearer and nearer. It is very real to me. The words have made a body for it and given it somewhere to walk.

If, at the time of writing this poem, I had found livelier words, words that could give me much more vividly its movements, the twitch and craning of its ears, the slight tremor of its hanging tongue and its breath making little clouds, its teeth bared in the cold, the snow-crumbs dropping from its pads as it lifts each one in turn, if I could have got the words for all this, the fox would probably be even more real and alive to me now, than it is as I read the poem. Still, it is there as it is. If I had not caught the real fox there in the words I would never have saved the poem. I would have thrown it into the waste-paper basket as I have thrown so many other hunts that did not get what I was after. As it is, every time I read the poem the fox comes up again out of the darkness and steps into my head. And I suppose that long after I am gone, as long as a copy of the poem exists, every time anyone reads it the fox will get up somewhere out in the darkness and come walking towards them.

# Imagining

Ted Hughes says that the most important thing when you are writing a poem is to 'imagine what you are writing about. See it and live it . . . Look at it, touch it, smell it, listen to it, turn yourself into it.' On this page there are suggestions for subjects to write about in this way.

Writing    **1**   As you look at this picture, imagine that you are 'in it'—right in one corner. Imagine what you can see, hear, and feel. Think the thoughts that pass through your head. When you have imagined it fully, write about it.

         **2**   Forget what the picture is 'really about'. Imagine that it is the pattern on a piece of material. Write a description of the pattern of the material: describe the shapes, the colours, and the texture of the material. If you can, use comparisons to make the description more vivid.

**Writing**

1. Look at the picture and imagine yourself into it. Imagine what you can hear, see, feel, smell, taste. Write about the experience.
2. Turn the picture upside down. Look at it not as a picture of something happening, but as a pattern. Describe the pattern as vividly as you can.

**Final version**

Look at the writing you have done about either of the pictures. Imagine that you are a reader who has not seen the picture and who does not know how the writing was done. Ask yourself: is the writing clear? Does it describe accurately the thoughts and feelings you had? Are there places where the meaning is not clear? Are there any ways in which you can make the writing more vivid? Think about these questions and then *reshape* your writing in any ways you think necessary.

# *Learning to think*

Now first of all I had better make it quite clear that I am going to talk about a certain kind of thinking. One of the odd wonderful things about this activity we call thinking is that to some extent everybody invents their own brand, has his own way of thinking, not only his own thoughts. You do not ever have to worry that you are not thinking properly—not unless you enter some very specialized job, where a very specialized kind of thinking is required. All you have to do really is think.

And thinking, as we know, is as natural as breathing—some sort of thinking is generally going on in us all the time. So what is all the fuss about? Well, the terrible fact is that though we are all more or less thinking of something or other all the time, some of us are thinking more and some less. Some of us are more energetic about it.

Just as some people are bustling about all the time, getting things done, while others just sit around—so it is inside people's minds—some brains are battling and working and remembering and puzzling things over all the time, or much of the time, and other brains are just lying down snoring and occasionally turning over. Now I am not speaking to that first kind. There is not much I can say to them except wish them good luck. It is to the lazy or secret minds that I am now speaking, and from my own experience I imagine this includes nineteen people out of every twenty. I am one of that clan myself and always have been.

At school, I was plagued by the idea that I really had much better thoughts than I could ever get into words. It was not that I could not find the words, or that the thoughts were too deep or too complicated for words. It was simply that when I tried to speak or write down the thoughts, those thoughts had vanished. All I had was a numb blank feeling, just as if somebody had asked me the name of Julius Caesar's eldest son, or said '7,283 times 6,956—quick. Think, think, think'. Now for one reason or another I became very interested in those thoughts of mine that I could never catch. Sometimes they were hardly what you could call a thought—they were a dim sort of feeling about something. They did not fit into any particular subject—history or arithmetic or anything of that sort, except perhaps English. I had the idea, which gradually grew on me, that these were the right sort of thoughts for essays, and yet probably not even essays. But for the most part they were useless to me because I could never get hold of them. Maybe when I was writing an essay I got the tail end of one, but that was not very satisfying.

Now maybe you can see what was happening. I was thinking all right, and even having thoughts that seemed interesting to me, but I could not keep hold of the thoughts, or fish them up when I wanted them. I would think this fact was something peculiar to me, and of interest to nobody else, if I did not know that most people have the same trouble. What thoughts they have are fleeting thoughts – just a flash of it, then gone – or, though they know they know something, or have ideas about something, they just cannot dig those ideas up when they are wanted. Their minds, in fact, seem out of their reach. That is a curious thing to say, but it is quite true.

There is the inner life, which is the world of final reality, the world of memory, emotion, imagination, intelligence, and natural common sense, and which goes on all the time, consciously or unconsciously, like the heart beat. There is also the thinking process by which we break into that inner life and capture answers and evidence to support the answers out of it. That process of raid, or persuasion, or ambush, or dogged hunting, or surrender, is the kind of thinking we have to learn and if we do not somehow learn it, then our minds lie in us like the fish in the pond of a man who cannot fish.

Now you see the kind of thinking I am talking about. Perhaps I ought not to call it thinking at all – it is just that we tend to call everything that goes on in our heads thinking. I am talking about whatever kind of trick or skill it is that enables us to catch those elusive or shadowy thoughts, and collect them together, and hold them still so we can get a really good look at them. I will illustrate what I mean with an example: If you were told, 'Think of your uncle' – how long could you hold the idea of your uncle in your head? Right, you imagine him. But then at once he reminds you of something else and you are thinking of that, he has gone into the background, if he has not altogether disappeared. Now get your uncle back. Imagine your uncle and nothing else – nothing whatsoever. After all, there is plenty to be going on with in your uncle. His eyes, what expression? His hair, where is it parted? How many waves has it? What is the exact shade? Or if he is bald, what does the skin feel like? His chin—just how is it? Look at it. As you can see, there is a great deal to your uncle—you could spend hours on him, if you could only keep him in your mind for hours; and when you have looked at him from head to foot, in your memory you have all the memories of what he has said and done, and all your own feelings about him and his sayings and doings. You could spend weeks on him, just holding him there in your mind, and examining the thoughts you have about him. I have exaggerated that, but you see straightaway that it is quite difficult to think about

your uncle and nothing but your uncle for more than a few seconds.
So how can you ever hope to collect all your thoughts about him.

At the same time you obviously could not do that with
everything that came into your head—grip hold of it with your
imagination, and never let it go till you had studied every grain of it.
It would not leave you any time to live. Nevertheless, it is possible
to do it for a time. I will illustrate the sort of thing I mean with a
poem called *View of a Pig*. In this poem, the poet stares at something
which is quite still, and collects the thoughts that concern it.

He does it quite rapidly and briefly, never lifting his eyes from
the pig. Obviously, he does not use every thought possible—he
chooses the thoughts that fit best together to make a poem. Here is
the poem: *View of a Pig*.


The pig lay on a barrow dead.
It weighed, they said, as much as three men.
Its eyes closed, pink white eyelashes
Its trotters stuck straight out.

Such weight and thick, pink bulk
Set in death seemed not just dead.
It was less than lifeless, further off.
It was like a sack of wheat.

I thumped it without feeling remorse.
One feels guilty insulting the dead,
Walking on graves. But this pig
Did not seem able to accuse.

It was too dead. Just so much
A poundage of lard and pork.
Its last dignity had entirely gone.
It was not a figure of fun.

Too dead now to pity.
To remember its life, din, stronghold
Of earthly pleasure as it had been,
Seemed a false effort, and off the point.

Too deadly factual. Its weight
Oppressed me—how could it be moved?
And the trouble of cutting it up!
The gash in its throat was shocking, but not pathetic.

Once I ran at a fair in the noise
To catch a greased piglet
That was faster and nimbler than a cat,
Its squeal was the rending of metal

Pigs must have hot blood, they feel like ovens,
Their bite is worse than a horse's—
They chop a half-moon clean out.
They eat cinders, dead cats.

Distinctions and admirations such
As this one was long finished with.
I stared at it a long time. They were going to scald it,
Scald it and scour it like a doorstep.

    Now where did the poet learn to settle his mind like that on to
one thing? It is a valuable thing to be able to do—but something you
are never taught at school, and not many people do it naturally. I am
not very good at it, but I did acquire some skill in it. Not in the
school, but while I was fishing. I fished in still water, with a float.
As you know, all a fisherman does is stare at his float for hours on
end. I have spent hundreds and hundreds of hours staring at a float –
a dot of red or yellow the size of a lentil, ten yards away. Those of
you who have never done it, might think it is a very drowsy
pastime. It is anything but that.

    All the little nagging impulses, that are normally distracting
your mind, dissolve. They have to dissolve if you are to go on
fishing. If they do not, then you cannot settle down: you get bored
and pack up in a bad temper. But once they have dissolved, you
enter one of the orders of bliss.

    Your whole being rests lightly on your float, but not drowsily:
very alert, so that the least twitch of the float arrives like an electric
shock. And you are not only watching the float. You are aware, in a
horizonless and slightly mesmerized way, like listening to the
double bass in orchestral music, of the fish below there in the dark.
At every moment your imagination is alarming itself with the size of
the thing slowly leaving the weeds and approaching your bait. Or
with the world of beauties down there, suspended in total ignorance
of you. And the whole purpose of this concentrated excitement, in
this arena of apprehension and unforeseeable events, is to bring up
some lovely solid thing like living metal from a world where
nothing exists but those inevitable facts which raise life out of
nothing and return it to nothing.

    So you see, fishing with a float is a sort of mental exercise in
concentration on a small point, while at the same time letting your
imagination work freely to collect everything that might concern
that still point: in this case the still point is the float and the things
that concern the float are all the fish you are busy imagining. It is not
very far from this, you see, to staring steadily at an imagined picture
or idea of my uncle and collecting all the thoughts about him that
seem to be roaming round my mind, or that come up to look at him.

# Concentrating and writing

1 Concentrate on the photograph in the way that Ted Hughes suggests.
2 After a few minutes, write down all the thoughts that have come into your head.
3 Concentrate on the picture again. Write down any further thoughts that you have.
4 Use your notes as the basis of a poem or piece of prose expressing your thoughts and feelings about the picture.

**Choosing your own subject**

Choose your own subject to write about. Here are some suggestions about simple subjects that you could choose:
  a a person whom you know well
  b an animal—pet, bird, insect
  c a machine or tool
  d a place with which you are familiar
Concentrate on it in the way that Ted Hughes suggests. Then write about it.

**Organizing your writing**

Look again at Ted Hughes' poem *View of a Pig*. Study the way in which he has arranged it on the page. You will notice that in most cases he seems to put a complete thought in a line. Each four-line verse contains a group of such thoughts. Choose one of your pieces of writing and organize it in a similar way.

# Leaves

Who's killed the leaves?
Me, says the apple, I've killed them all.
Fat as a bomb or a cannonball
I've killed the leaves

Who sees them drop?
Me, says the pear, they will leave me all bare
So all the people can point and stare.
I see them drop.

Who'll catch their blood?
Me, me, me, says the marrow, the marrow.
I'll get so rotund that they'll need a wheelbarrow.
I'll catch their blood.

Who'll make their shroud?
Me, says the swallow, there's just time enough
Before I must pack all my spools and be off.
I'll make their shroud.

Who'll dig their grave?
Me, says the river, with the power of the clouds
A brown deep grave I'll dig under my floods.
I'll dig their grave.

Who'll be their parson?
Me, says the Crow, for it is well-known
I study the bible right down to the bone.
I'll be their parson.

Who'll be chief mourner?
Me, says the wind, I will cry through the grass
The people will pale and go cold when I pass.
I'll be chief mourner.

Who'll carry the coffin?
Me, says the sunset, the whole world will weep
To see me lower it into the deep.
I'll carry the coffin.

Who'll sing a psalm?
Me, says the tractor, with my gear grinding glottle
I'll plough up the stubble and sing through my throttle.
I'll sing the psalm.

Who'll toll the bell?
Me, says the robin, my song in October
Will tell the still gardens the leaves are over.
I'll toll the bell.

# There Came a Day

There came a day that caught the summer
Wrung its neck
Plucked it
And ate it.

Now what shall I do with the trees?
The day said, the day said.
Strip them bare, strip them bare.
Let's see what is really there.

And what shall I do with the sun?
The day said, the day said.
Roll him away till he's cold and small.
He'll come back rested if he comes back at all.

And what shall I do with the birds?
The day said, the day said.
The birds I've frightened, let them flit,
I'll hang out pork for the brave tomtit.

And what shall I do with the seed?
The day said, the day said.
Bury it deep, see what it's worth.
See if it can stand the earth.

What shall I do with the people?
The day said, the day said.
Stuff them with apple and blackberry pie—
They'll love me then till the day they die.

There came this day and he was autumn.
His mouth was wide
And red as a sunset.
His tail was an icicle.

# Pattern poems

Both of these poems are written according to a pattern. *Leaves* is based on a well-known nursery rhyme, *Who Killed Cock Robin?*:

Who killed Cock Robin?
    I, said the sparrow,
    with my bow and arrow,
I killed Cock Robin.

Who saw him die?
    I, said the fly
    with my little eye,
I saw him die.
    etc. etc.

The poem then goes through the ceremonies that happen when someone has died, but it changes them to talk about autumn and not about Cock Robin.

*There Came a Day* has a simpler pattern: except for the first and last verses, each verse begins with a question:

What shall I do with the _____?
The day said, the day said.

A pattern is a good simple way of organizing a poem. It helps you to put your thoughts and ideas down on the page in a simple but striking way.

Write a pattern poem. Choose your own subject and pattern —or use one of the patterns that Ted Hughes has used.

# Hands

Your hands were strange—huge.
A farmer's joke: 'still got your bloody great hands!'
You used them with as little regard
As old iron tools—as if their creased, glossed, crocodile leather
Were nerveless, like an African's footsoles.

When the barbed wire tightening hum-rigid
Snapped and leaped through your grip
You flailed your fingers like a caned boy, and laughed:
'Barbarous wire!' then just ignored them
As the half-inch deep, cross-hand rips dried.

And when your grasp nosed bullocks, prising their mouths
   wide,
So they dropped to their knees
I understood again
How the world of half-ton hooves, and horns,
And hides heedless as cedar-boarding, comes to be manageable.

Hands more of a piece with your tractor
Than with their own nerves,
Having no more compunction than dung-forks,
But suave as warm oil inside the wombs of ewes,
And monkey delicate

At that cigarette
Which glowed patient through all your labours
Nursing the one in your lung
To such strength, it squeezed your strength to water
And stopped you.

Your hands lie folded, estranged from all they have done
And as they have never been, and startling—
So slender, so taper, so white,
Your mother's hands suddenly in your hands—
In a final strangeness of elegance.

# A Memory

Your bony white bowed back, in a singlet,
Powerful as a horse,
Bowed over an upturned sheep
Shearing under the East chill through-door draught
In the cave-dark barn, sweating and freezing—
Flame-crimson face, drum-guttural African curses
As you bundled the sheep
Like tying some oversize, overweight, spilling bale
Through its adjustments of position

The attached cigarette, bent at its glow
Preserving its pride of ash
Through all your suddenly savage, suddenly gentle
Masterings of the animal

You were like a collier, a face-worker
In a dark hole of obstacle
Heedless of your own surfaces
Inching by main strength into the solid hour,
Bald, arch-wrinkled, weathered dome bowed
Over your cigarette comfort

Till you stretched erect through a groan
Letting a peeled sheep leap free

Then nipped the bud of stub from your lips
And with glove-huge, grease-glistening carefulness
Lit another at it

# Thinking about the poems

## Hands

In this poem Ted Hughes writes about a man he knew well by describing his hands and the way in which he used and treated them. When you have read the poem, compare the first and last verses. They are very different from each other. What has caused the change? How did Ted Hughes feel about the farmer and what happened to him? How do you know?

## A Memory

lines 1–9    What is the man doing? Where is he? What does Ted Hughes compare the place to? What is the man doing while he is working? What does it sound like?

lines 10–13  How does the farmer's handling of the sheep change from time to time?

lines 14–19  What else does Ted Hughes compare the farmer and his actions to?

lines 20–23  What do the farmer and the sheep do at the end?

Does the poem give you a vivid picture of what is happening? Which parts strike you as being particularly clear and easy to imagine? Why are these sections effective?

**Your own writing**

1  *Hands*: choose a person you know well. Concentrate your mind on that person and, in particular, remember his or her hands. Try to picture those hands in your mind: their colour, their size and shape. Are they large or small? Fat or thin? Wrinkled or smooth? Remember the typical ways in which those hands move – are they strong? Nervous? Fidgety? Calm? When you have a clear picture of the hands in your mind, write a description of them. Try to describe the person's whole character simply by writing about his or her hands.

2  *A Memory*: choose a person you know well. Fix your concentration on that person. Think of him or her in a typical situation or activity: doing something which you have often seen him or her doing. Form a picture of that in your mind. Now write about it.

# Outsiders

*The Scream* by Edvard Munch

# Cruel and unfair

*Stephen is at school in Ireland towards the end of the nineteenth century. It is a church school and discipline is the responsibility of the 'prefect of studies', Father Dolan. He has visited Stephen's class and punished a boy for not working hard enough. The punishment is to be hit on the hand with a pandybat – a leather strap.*

At your work, all of you! shouted the prefect of studies. We want no lazy idle loafers here, lazy idle little schemers. At your work, I tell you. Father Dolan will be in to see you every day. Father Dolan will be in tomorrow.

He poked one of the boys in the side with the pandybat, saying:

– You, boy! When will Father Dolan be in again?

– Tomorrow, sir, said Tom Furlong's voice.

– Tomorrow and tomorrow and tomorrow, said the prefect of studies. Make up your minds for that. Every day Father Dolan. Write away. You, boy, who are you?

Stephen's heart jumped suddenly.

– Dedalus, sir.

– Why are you not writing like the others?

– I . . . my . . .

He could not speak with fright.

– Why is he not writing, Father Arnall?

– He broke his glasses, said Father Arnall, and I exempted him from work.

– Broke? What is this I hear? What is this? Your name is? said the prefect of studies.

– Dedalus, sir.

– Out here, Dedalus. Lazy little schemer. I see schemer in your face. Where did you break your glasses?

Stephen stumbled into the middle of the class, blinded by fear and haste.

– Where did you break your glasses? repeated the prefect of studies.

– The cinderpath, sir.

– Hoho! The cinderpath! cried the prefect of studies. I know that trick. Lazy idle little loafer! Broke my glasses! An old schoolboy trick! Out with your hand this moment!

Stephen closed his eyes and held out in the air his trembling hand with the palm upwards. He felt the prefect of studies touch it for a moment at the fingers to straighten it and then the swish of the sleeve of the soutane as the pandybat was lifted to strike. A hot burning stinging tingling blow like the loud crack of a broken stick made his trembling hand crumple together like a leaf in the fire: and at the sound and the pain scalding tears were driven into his eyes. His whole body was shaking with fright, his arm was shaking and his crumpled burning livid hand shook like a loose leaf in the air A cry sprang to his lips, a prayer to be let off. But though the tears scalded his eyes and his limbs quivered with pain and fright he held back the hot tears and the cry that scalded his throat.

– Other hand! shouted the prefect of studies.

Stephen drew back his maimed and quivering right arm and held out his left hand. The soutane sleeve swished again as the pandybat was lifted and a loud crashing sound and a fierce maddening tingling burning pain made his hand shrink together with the palms and fingers in a livid quivering mass. The scalding water burst forth from his eyes and, burning with shame and agony and fear, he drew back his shaking arm in terror and burst out into a whine of pain. His body shook with a palsy of fright and in shame and rage he felt the scalding cry come from his throat and the scalding tears falling out of his eyes and down his flaming cheeks.

– Kneel down! cried the prefect of studies.

Stephen knelt down quickly pressing his beaten hands to his sides. To think of them beaten and swollen with pain all in a moment made him feel so sorry for them as if they were not his own but someone else's that he felt sorry for. And as he knelt, calming the last sobs in his throat and feeling the burning tingling pain pressed into his sides, he thought of the hands which he had held out in the air with the palms up and of the firm touch of the prefect of studies when he had steadied the shaking fingers and of the beaten swollen reddened mass of palm and fingers that shook helplessly in the air.

– Get at your work, all of you, cried the prefect of studies from the door. Father Dolan will be in every day to see if any boy, any lazy idle little loafer wants flogging. Every day. Every day.

The door closed behind him.

The hushed class continued to copy out the themes. Father Arnall rose from his seat and went among them, helping the boys with gentle words and telling them the mistakes they had made. His voice was very gentle and soft. Then he returned to his seat and said to Fleming and Stephen:

– You may return to your places, you two.

Fleming and Stephen rose and, walking to their seats, sat down. Stephen, scarlet with shame, opened a book quickly with one weak hand and bent down upon it, his face close to the page.

It was unfair and cruel because the doctor has told him not to read without his glasses and he had written home to his father that morning to send him a new pair. And Father Arnall had said that he need not study till the new glasses came. Then to be called a schemer before the class and to be pandied. It was cruel and unfair.

**James Joyce,** *Portrait of the Artist as a Young Man*

**Questions to think and talk about**

1 Discuss Father Dolan's attitude to the boys. Why do you think such a man worked in the school?
2 In what ways to you think the incident affected Stephen's attitude to the school?
3 If you were Stephen, how would you feel and what would you do?
4 Pandybats are now no longer used, but are there occasions today in which schools are unfair to pupils and make them feel outsiders?

**Writing**

Think of an occasion from your own life when you have been unfairly treated or have been made to feel an outsider. Remember what it felt like. Write about it, either as a true story, or as part of a story you make up.

# Pretty Boy Floyd

Come and gather 'round me, children,
A story I will tell
About Pretty Boy Floyd, the outlaw,
Oklahoma knew him well.

It was in the town of Shawnee
On a Saturday afternoon,
His wife beside him in the wagon,
As into town they rode.

There a deputy sheriff approached him
In a manner rather rude,
Using vulgar words of anger,
And his wife, she overheard.

Pretty Boy grabbed a log chain,
The deputy grabbed his gun,
And in the fight that followed
He laid that deputy down.

Then he took to the trees and the timber
To live a life of shame,
Every crime in Oklahoma
Was added to his name.

Yes, he took to the river bottom
Along the river shore,
And Pretty Boy found a welcome
At every farmer's door.

The paper said that Pretty Boy
Had robbed a bank each day,

While he was sitting in some farmhouse,
Three hundred miles away.

There's many a starving farmer
The same old story told,
How the outlaw paid their mortgage
And saved their little home.

Others tell you 'bout a stranger
That come to beg a meal,
And underneath his napkin
Left a thousand-dollar bill.

It was in Oklahoma City,
It was on a Christmas Day,
There came a whole carload of groceries
With a note to say:

'You say that I'm an outlaw,
You say that I'm a thief,
Here's a Christmas dinner
For the families on relief.'

Yes, as through this world I've rambled
I've seen lots of funny men,
Some will rob you with a six gun,
And some with a fountain pen.

But as through your life you travel,
Wherever you may roam,
You won't never see no outlaw
Drive a family from their home.

**Woodie Guthrie**

Questions
1 What is an outlaw?
2 Why did Pretty Boy Floyd attack the deputy sheriff?
3 What did each of them use in the fight?
4 Where did it happen?
5 Where did Floyd go?
6 Why did the farmers like him?
7 How did he 'pay' for meals he was given?
8 What did Floyd do one Christmas?
9 How can a man 'rob you . . . with a fountain pen'?
10 What does the last verse say in favour of outlaws?

# A menace to society

A     When Bill Fletcher was sentenced to eight years, the judge called him a 'menace to society': his immediate crime was stealing a ten-shilling note, but he had spent forty-four of his fifty-seven years in penal institutions, since he was sent to an approved school at the age of seven. The total value of his thefts amounts to under £40. From 1939 to 1971 he spent *a total* of seven months as a free man.

B     'I have been asked what lessons I have learnt from being inside. First Borstal taught me how to blow a safe, and it taught me what sadism, cruelty and real hatred were, such as I had not known before. The approved school, as it was called in those days, will always remain in my memory. You were forced to be a thief or you got beaten up. Of the boys who were with me then, three have been hanged for murder and two are doing life sentences for it. I learned how to exist by craft and cunning, because that is the only way to exist.

      Prison taught me what real terror is, the terror of being helpless when people hate you. I do not think I will really ever get over that feeling of terror, knowing what the authorities could do to a man like me and can still do to this day, because with a record you are never out of their clutches. My deepest impression of Dartmoor was my two and a half years in solitary confinement when I even went outside doing exercises in a cage, like a trapped animal. Loneliness is all you have to live with in prison. No one who hasn't experienced it can have any idea what it means to be in solitary confinement.

      These are some of the lessons I learnt in prison. What I learnt most of all was a dread of the human race.

C     I will try to explain the state you are in when you come out of prison. I am dealing now with a man like myself who has no home, no friends, no money, and only the clothes that the prison gives him if he has served a four-year sentence or over. You receive nowadays: one suit of clothes, one macintosh, one pair of shoes, two shirts, two vests, two pairs of socks, underwear, one razor, two handkerchiefs and one holdall plus £4 and a railway warrant to wherever you are going.* The Prison Governor gives you his best wishes, and then you have to start out on your own to live in this strange new world. The first thing that gets you is the noise and movement of traffic. Within an hour you feel a nervous wreck, for the pace of life is like nothing you ever experienced inside. You are in a crowd of people, yet you are lonely, lost and bewildered. You will look for a shop where there is only a man serving. I find that, even now, if I am alone, I will only go into a cafe if I have been taken there two or three times by someone; otherwise I will always go to a railway station to get something to eat from the trollies on the platforms. I have never in my life been shopping for such things as suits, overcoats, socks, shirts, ties, shoes, or any form of clothing, for the simple reason that I have never been out long enough to need new clothes.

You can only lead the life you know. You have to acclimatize yourself to strange new conditions, and it takes time and infinite patience so that many people go back inside again.

D  Two years ago I decided that I could never make a go of it outside. There seemed no point in trying any further. So I took the necessary steps: I used a jemmy on a telephone kiosk which was alarmed up, and waited for the police to come. Within two minutes I was arrested.

When I came before the magistrate again he decided, because of my past record, he could not give me a big enough sentence. So I was sent to Wandsworth prison to await sentence at Hereford Quarter Sessions. I had already pleaded guilty and was glad they intended to try to get what I wanted, a long sentence. I wished just to settle down to the only life I felt that I could live with any chance of happiness at all.

I was in for the biggest shock of my life. I was given no opportunity whatsoever to say anything for myself, either to help or to hinder, for the judge would not even listen to the charges being read out. He said: 'You are John William Fletcher?'

I said, 'Yes my lord.'

He said, 'I have read your record, and I am amazed at it. I think I can say this, you have had every form of punishment that it is possible for you to have,' and he named them all: industrial school, training ship, Borstal, imprisonment, penal servitude, preventive detention, probation orders – 'and that shocks me. There is only one thing that I can do in this case, and that is to give you the only thing that you have not had: an absolute discharge.'

*The Observer,* 11 June 1972

*In 1981 a homeless man received £46.65

# In Coventry

In Coventry, that ruddled city,
Under a metal, shunting sky,
I sat in the cracked cathedral,
The holiday-makers limping by.

Christ hung down like a hawk-moth
    caterpillar,
Down his cheeks ran woollen tears.
On the chapel gate his crown of thorns
Was made by the Royal Engineers.

As I walked through the glittering
    Precinct
All the retablos burned like gold.
I heard a gear-change of bones
    behind me.
I saw a man lying, flat-out, cold.

He hit the slabs as though he'd been
    sand-bagged.
A thicket of blood sprang on his face.
We looked for a seat to lay him out on,
But man must keep moving in that place.

The rain fell down the concrete mountain.
Four friends came back, breathing hard.
Pull yourself together, Taff, they chunnered.
But his legs were butter and his face
    was lard.

Taff, don't let us down, they were saying.
Taff looked dead and half-buried already,
As on a river of whisky he'd taken
The quickest way out of Coventry city.

Later, on a weir of steps, I saw him
Stumbling, alone; past hopes and fears.
The blood and hair on his jagged brow
Held in place by the engineers.

**Charles Causley**

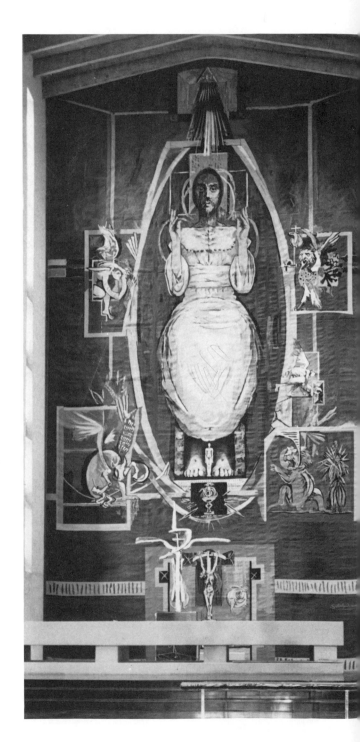

# I am

I am: yet what I am none cares or knows,
   My friends forsake me like a memory lost;
I am the self-consumer of my woes,
   They rise and vanish in oblivious host,
Like shades in love and death's oblivion lost;
And yet I am, and live with shadows tost

Into the nothingness of scorn and noise,
   Into the living sea of waking dreams,
Where there is neither sense of life nor joys,
   But the vast shipwreck of my life's esteems;
And e'en the dearest – that I loved the best –
Are strange – nay, rather stranger than the rest.

I long for scenes where man has never trod,
   A place where woman never smiled or wept;
There to abide with my Creator, God,
   And sleep as I in childhood sweetly slept:
Untroubled and untroubling where I lie,
The grass below – above the vaulted sky.

**John Clare**

# *Extra lesson*

**Germany 1934**

The school bell rang. At the last tone, Teacher Neudorf closed the book and stood up. Slowly, in thought, he walked towards us. He cleared his throat and said: 'The lesson is over – but please stay a little longer; I want to tell you a story. Anyone who wants to can go home, though.'

We looked at each other quizzically.

Herr Neudorf stepped to the window, turning his back to us. From his jacket pocket he drew a pipe and began to fill it, looking at the trees in the playground all the while.

Noisily we collected our things. We prepared our briefcases and satchels. But no one left the classroom. We all waited.

Awkwardly, Herr Neudorf lit his pipe. With obvious enjoyment he blew a few puffs against the windows. Only then did he turn to face us. He surveyed the rows of seats. When he saw that all were still filled, he nodded to us with a smile.

All eyes focused on Herr Neudorf. We didn't talk. From the hall came the sounds of other classes. In one of the back benches someone shuffled his feet.

Herr Neudorf walked to the front row. He sat on one of the desks. His pipe glowing, he looked at each of us in turn and blew the smoke over our heads to the window.

We stared at our teacher, tense and expectant.

At last he began to speak in a calm, soft voice. 'Lately, you've heard a lot about Jews, haven't you?' We nodded. 'Well, today I also have a reason to talk to you about Jews.'

We leaned forward to hear better. A few propped their chins on their schoolbags. There wasn't a sound.

Herr Neudorf directed a blue cloud of sweet-smelling smoke up to the ceiling. After a pause, he continued, 'Two thousand years ago all Jews lived in the land which is now called Palestine; the Jews call it Israel.

'The Romans governed the country through their governors and prefects. But the Jews did not want to submit to foreign rule and they rebelled against the Romans. The Romans smashed the uprising and in the year 70 after the birth of Christ destroyed the Second Temple in Jerusalem. The leaders of the revolt were banished to Spain or the Rhineland. A generation later, the Jews dared to rise again. This time the Romans razed Jerusalem to the ground. The Jews fled or were banished. They scattered over the whole earth.

'Years passed. Many gained wealth and standing. Then came the Crusades.

'Heathens had conquered the Holy Land and kept Christians from the holy places. Eloquent priests demanded the liberation of the Holy Grave; inflamed by their words, thousands of people assembled.

'But some declared, "What is the use of marching against the infidels in the Holy Land while there are infidels living in our midst?"

'Thus began the persecution of the Jews. In many places they were herded together; they were murdered and burned. They were dragged by force to be baptized; those who refused were tortured.

'Hundreds of Jews took their own lives to escape massacre. Those who could escape did so.

'When the Crusades were over, impoverished sovereigns who had taken part in them had their Jewish subjects imprisoned and executed without trials and claimed their possessions.

'Again, many Jews fled, this time to the East. They found refuge in Poland and Russia. But in the last century, there, too, they began to be persecuted.

'The Jews were forced to live in ghettos, in isolated sections of towns. They were not allowed to take up so called "honest" professions: they could not become craftsmen nor were they allowed to own houses or land. They were only allowed to work in trade and at money lending.'

The teacher paused, his pipe had gone out. He placed it in the groove for pens and pencils. He got off the desk and wandered about the classroom. He polished his glasses and continued:

'The Old Testament of the Christians is also the Holy Scripture of the Jews; they call it Torah, which means "instruction". In the Torah is written down what God commanded Moses. The Jews have thought a great deal about the Torah and its commandments. How the laws of the Torah are to be interpreted they have put down in another very great work – the Talmud, which means "study".

'Orthodox Jews still live by the law of the Torah. And that is not easy. The Torah, for instance, forbids the Jew to light a fire on the Sabbath or to eat the meat of unclean animals such as pigs.

'The Torah prophesies the Jews' fate. If they break the holy laws, they will be persecuted and must flee, until the Messiah leads them back to their Promised Land, there to create His Kingdom among them. Because Jews did not believe Jesus to be the true Messiah, because they regarded him as an impostor like many before him, they crucified him. And to this day many people have not forgiven them for this. They believe the most absurd things about Jews; some only wait for the day when they can persecute them again.

'There are many people who do not like Jews. Jews strike them as strange and sinister; they believe them capable of everything bad just because they don't know them well enough!'

Attentively we followed the account. It was so quiet that we could hear the soles of Herr Neudorf's shoes creak. Everyone looked at him; only Friedrich looked down at his hands.

'Jews are accused of being crafty and sly. How could they be anything else? Someone who must always live in fear of being tormented and hunted must be very strong in his soul to remain an upright human being.

'It is claimed that the Jews are avaricious and deceitful. Must they not be both? Again and again, they have been robbed and dispossessed; again and again, they had to leave everything they owned behind. They have discovered that in case of need money is the only way to secure life and safety.

'But one thing even the worst Jew-haters have to concede – the Jews are a very capable people! Only able people can survive two thousand years of persecution.

'By always accomplishing more and doing it better than the people they lived among, the Jews gained esteem and importance again and again. Many great scholars and artists were and are Jews.

'If today, or tomorrow, you should see Jews being mistreated, reflect on one thing – Jews are human beings, human beings like us!'

Without glancing at us, Herr Neudorf took up his pipe. He scraped the ashes out of the bowl and lit the remaining tobacco. After a few puffs, he said, 'Now I am sure you will want to know why I have told you all this, eh?'

He walked to Friedrich's seat and put a hand on his shoulder.

'One of us will leave our school today. It appears that Friedrich Schneider may no longer come to our school; he must change to a Jewish school because he is of the Jewish faith.

'That Friedrich has to attend a Jewish school is no punishment, but only a change. I hope you will understand that and remain Friedrich's friends, just as I will remain his friend even though he will no longer be in my class. Friedrich may need good friends.'

Herr Neudorf turned Friedrich around by his shoulder. 'I wish you all the best, Friedrich!' the teacher said, 'and *Auf Wiedersehen!*'

Friedrich bent his head. In a low voice he replied, '*Auf Wiedersehen!*'

With quick steps Herr Neudorf hurried to the front of the class. He jerked up his right arm, the hand straight out at eye level, and said: 'Heil Hitler!'

We jumped up and returned the greeting in the same way.

**Hans Peter Richter,** *Friedrich*

*The events described in this story were part of the process in Nazi Germany which ended with the killing of six million Jews. The Jews were first separated from non-Jews. Their businesses were destroyed or confiscated. Later they were put into concentration camps where they were systematically killed. The whole process was accompanied by a carefully worked out propaganda campaign in which the German people were indoctrinated to believe that Jews were inferior to other people and that they were responsible for Germany's problems. All this was done under the leadership of Adolf Hitler.*

# Ned Kelly

The next four pages contain the raw materials for a number of different storytelling activities. The materials are based on the life of the Australian outlaw Ned Kelly. There are suggestions for activities at the end of this section.

## Kelly's life

Kelly's
horse-brand

1854    Edward Kelly born at Beveridge, near Melbourne.
Father: John 'Red' Kelly, ex-convict, Irish.
Mother: Ellen Quinn, immigrant, Irish.

1866    Moved to Eleven Mile Creek, near Greta, north-east Victoria.

1868    Ned Kelly sentenced to 6 months' imprisonment for assault. (There was an argument about a horse and he attacked the man he was arguing with.)

1869    Sentenced to three years in prison for receiving a stolen horse.

1872–5 Worked as timber cutter and did other jobs in the hills known as the Wombat Ranges.

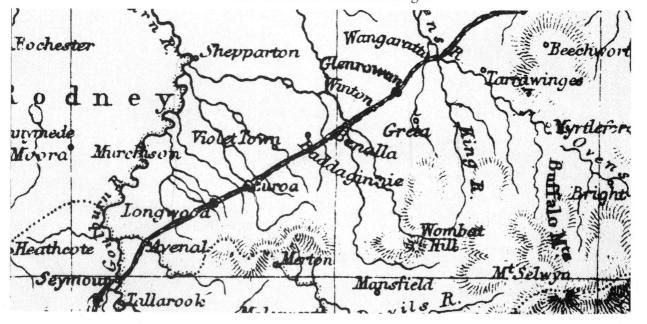

1877   Arrested for drunkenness but later released.

1878   New policeman, Constable Fitzpatrick, takes over Greta *Scott*
police station. Decides to clean the district up. Goes to Kelly
homestead and returns injured (and smelling of drink).

As a result of Fitzpatrick's report, Ned Kelly's mother is
sentenced to three years in prison, for assault. (Fitzpatrick
was later dismissed from the police for lying.) Ned Kelly
takes to the hills as an outlaw. He is accompanied by Dan
Kelly, Joe Byrne, and Steve Hart: all expert shots and
horsemen.

*26 October*: Ned Kelly shoots and kills three policemen
(Lonigan, Scanlon, Kennedy) who have been sent to bring
him in. A fourth, McIntyre, is allowed to go free.

*December*: The Kelly gang hold up the National Bank in
Euroa, Victoria, and steal £2,000.

1879   *The attack on Jerilderie*: The Kelly Gang lock up the police in
their own police station, steal their uniforms, and dressed as
police spend two days in the town. They hold up the Bank of
New South Wales and steal £2,000.

1880   Kelly Gang attacks small town of Glenrowan. They take
hostages and hold them in the Glenrowan Inn. The police
move in and the 'Siege of Glenrowan' begins. Joe Byrne shot
and killed. Kelly puts on home-made iron armour and
confronts police. The armour stops bullets, but he is shot in
his unprotected legs and taken prisoner. Glenrowan Inn
burned down and rest of gang killed.

*28th October*: Trial of Ned Kelly.

*11th November*: Ned Kelly hanged.

Still from *The Last Outlaw*
(Pegasus Productions)
showing Ned Kelly about to be
hanged.

| Kelly's statement at his trial | It is not that I fear death; I fear it as little as to drink a cup of tea. I do not pretend to have led a blameless life or that one fault justifies another: but the public, when judging a case like mine, should remember that the darkest life may have a bright side, and after the worst has been said against man, he may, if he is heard, tell a different story in his own rough way. Let the hand of the law strike me down if it will; but I ask that my story be heard and considered – not that I wish to avoid anything the law may think necessary to carry out justice or win a word of pity from anybody. If my lips teach the public that men are made mad by bad treatment, and if the police are taught that they may exasperate to madness men they persecute and ill-treat, my life will not be entirely thrown away. People who live in large towns have no idea of the tyrannical conduct of the police in country places far removed from the court. |
|---|---|

# The Ballad of Edward Kelly

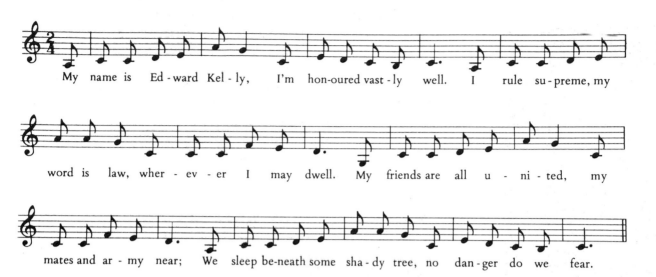

My name is Ed-ward Kel-ly, I'm hon-oured vast-ly well. I rule su-preme, my word is law, wher-ev-er I may dwell. My friends are all u-ni-ted, my mates and ar-my near; We sleep be-neath some sha-dy tree, no dan-ger do we fear.

Now the first of my adventures was through my sister dear,
Who was grossly insulted and put in bodily fear;
And when I came to hear of this it made my heart to ache;
I took to the hills to have revenge, all for my sister's sake.

Oh I am young and in my prime, I'm twenty-four years old.
I spent some time in vanity among young girls so bold;
But now I am a-robbing, and loudly my guns do roar.
'Twas there I shot poor Kennedy, which grieved my heart full sore.

In Mansfield that fair township where I was bred and born,
Oft times have I roamed those hills from dark till early dawn,
But now I am a-robbing upon the Queen's Highway;
We fight the traps, and rob the banks and quickly slip away.

Now the troopers they are all sent out to search the country round,
To bring in this notorious gang, but the Kellys can't be found.
The Kellys are in the ridges, the police in ranks abound;
The price upon my head, my boys, is now one thousand pound.

*The Queensland Pocket Songbook*

*Kelly and horse* by Sidney Nolan

**Activities**

1 Write the story of Ned Kelly's life as *he* saw it. (Write it as 'I').

2 Write the story of his life as it might have been told in newspaper reports in 1878, 1879, and 1880.

3 Write further verses for the Ballad of Edward Kelly, describing other exploits of the Kelly Gang.

4 Write a play about the life of Ned Kelly.

5 Two people hold opposite views about Ned Kelly. One believes that he was a vicious and drunken thief and murderer: the other that he was a man forced by injustice and persecution into becoming an outlaw. They argue. Write their argument as a conversation.

6 Make up a 'Ned Kelly File', consisting of statements about him by people who knew him and witnessed some of the things he did.

# Money, money, money

Which of these people do you think should be paid the most?
Why?
Some people say that everyone who works should earn the same amount.
What do you think?

# *Ambition*

*Joe is sitting in a café, looking out of the window at the street outside.*

At the moment the waitress brought the tea something happened which changed my whole life.

Parked by a solicitor's office opposite the café was a green Aston-Martin tourer, low-slung, with cycle-type mudguards. It had the tough, functional smartness of the good British sports car; it's a quality which is difficult to convey without using the terms of the advertising copywriter – made by craftsmen, thoroughbred, and so on – I can only say that it was a beautiful piece of engineering and leave it at that. Pre-war it would have cost as much as three baby saloons; it wasn't the sort of vehicle for business or for family outings but quite simply a rich man's toy.

As I was admiring it a young man and a girl came out of the solicitor's office. The young man was turning the ignition key when the girl said something to him and after a moment's argument he put up the windscreen. The girl smoothed his hair for him; I found the gesture disturbing in an odd way – it was again as if a barrier had been removed, but this time by an act of reason.

The ownership of the Aston-Martin automatically placed the young man in a social class far above mine; but that ownership was simply a question of money. The girl, with her even suntan and her fair hair cut short in a style too simple to be anything else but expensive, was as far beyond my reach as the car. But her ownership, too, was simply a question of money, of the price of the diamond ring on her left hand. This seems all too obvious; but it was the kind of truth which until that moment I'd only grasped theoretically.

The Aston-Martin started with a deep, healthy roar. As it passed the café in the direction of St. Clair Road I noticed the young man's olive linen shirt and bright silk neckerchief. The collar of the shirt was tucked inside the jacket; he wore the rather theatrical ensemble with a matter-of-fact nonchalance. Everything about him was easy and loose but not tired or sloppy. He had an undistinguished face with a narrow forehead and mousy hair cut short with no oil on it. It was a rich man's face, smooth with assurance and good living.

He hadn't ever had to work for anything he wanted; it had all been given him. The salary which I'd been so pleased about, an increase from Grade Ten to Grade Nine, would seem a pittance to him. The suit in which I fancied myself so much – my best suit – would seem cheap and nasty to him. He wouldn't have a *best* suit; all his clothes would be the best.

For a moment I hated him. I saw myself, compared with him, as the Town Hall clerk, the subordinate pen-pusher, halfway to being a zombie, and I tasted the sourness of envy. Then I rejected it. Not on moral grounds; but because I felt then, and still do, that envy's a small and squalid vice – the convict sulking because a fellow-prisoner's been given a bigger helping of skilly. This didn't abate the fierceness of my longing. I wanted an Aston-Martin, I wanted a three-guinea linen shirt, I wanted a girl with a Riviera suntan – these were my rights, I felt, a signed and sealed legacy.

As I watched the tail-end of the Aston-Martin with its shiny new G.B. plate go out of sight I remembered the secondhand Austin Seven which the Efficient Zombie, Dufton's Chief Treasurer, had just treated himself to. That was the most the local government had to offer me; it wasn't enough. I made my choice then and there: I was going to enjoy all the luxuries which that young man enjoyed. I was going to collect that legacy. It was as clear and compelling as the sense of vocation which doctors and missionaries are supposed to experience, though in my instance of course the call ordered me to do good to myself not others.

**John Braine,** *Room at the Top*

| Questions to think and talk about | | |
|---|---|---|
| | 1 | What are Joe's feelings about the car? |
| | 2 | What impression do you get of the girl? |
| | 3 | How does Joe feel about the man? |
| | 4 | How does this make him feel about himself? |
| | 5 | Why does he refuse to feel envy? |
| | 6 | What job does Joe do? |
| | 7 | What does he think of his job after watching the couple in the car? |
| | 8 | By the end of the extract what has he decided? |
| | 9 | What general impression do you get of Joe as a person? |
| | 10 | Do you think that a lot of people feel and think like him? |

Writing

*Room at the Top* was written in the 1950s, and all the details in the extract are typical of that period. In what ways would the scene be different if it were taking place today? Could it take place today? Write a similar story about ambition in a present day setting.

# Growing up in the 1920s

*Joe Bill Lightfoot was born in Cumbria in 1908. He grew up in a time of great poverty. He was interviewed about his life and his memories by the writer Melvyn Bragg. This is a transcript of what he said in the interview.*

Always hungry. I got very embarrassed sometimes, but it happened all the way through the line. A person or a child, of course I'll take the child, what I mean to say, up to he was fifteen, up till he was sixteen even, he didn't know what a pair of shoes was. All clogs. Off Willie Park. I think they cost seven and sixpence. Well I never had a new suit – when I was a boy, up till I started at the pit at fourteen years of age. The only thing I got, the only thing I had, a jersey and what they call, a sort of one of those hard collars with a stud in. I don't know whether you've seen them studs, have you. And of course you can twist the end bit anywhere for to get in the hole. Well of course they were called celluloid collars and of course you could wash them. And the only pants I had was a pair cut down, either from my father's or from a pair she had got given off somebody, and a handkerchief. You just didn't know what handkerchiefs were. Bit of old shirt tail to put in your pocket. And if you sort of lost that well it was this – finger and thumb. Well at about fifteen and a half I got my first long pants. At Redmayne's. First long pants of blue serge and a pair of tawny red shoes. Well like you know how I felt. Shirt and a collar.

The place we lived in up New Street. Well of course in them days they were all sort of bungalow-type. Two rooms. There was my father and mother's room, and then the one room for all the five of us kids. Only one bed in the room and the rest on shakky downs. Just a mattress. Only a mattress just put on the ground. Of course that was for the three boys. And that acted as a bed. As far as lavatory was concerned, all dry at the bottom of the garden with a bucket in. Who used to get that job, a filthy thing? Me. Joe Muggins. And the only place you could empty that, like we had a garden maybe the length of this, maybe twenty-five yards, and the only place you could empty that bucket was to dig a hole, empty it in, and then put the bucket back again. Then we had the ash pit. Of course you would know about the ash pit. In Wigton when they come round with the cart, go round the ash pits and put the ashes in. It was a sort of hole. It protects the lavatory. So Dave Armstrong used to empty that with his horse and cart, but that's the only thing we had. And bluebottles and midges, I never saw anything like it in all my life. I've seen Water Street there, you couldn't move. It was hose-piped every Tuesday. Fetching the cattle in and doing their jobs all over the street, all the sheep and that, all coming down Water Street. Filthy. Never saw anything like it.

And as I say it was rough. As as far as meat was concerned, I know meat was cheap, but you just couldn't buy it. So therefore what we used to have, either dry bread and jam or butter and bread. If you got butter on your bread, you didn't get any jam. If you got jam on your bread, you didn't get any butter. If you fried, and very rare, a little bit of bacon or something, then when the fat was cold you put that on your bread. But Woodbines were twopence a packet. Sugar a penny halfpenny a pound. Twenty-four eggs for a shilling. Old Billy Tut used to come up to Bolton – Fresh herring, fresh herring, at the top of his voice. And they were all in barrels. Lovely herrings. Maybe twenty-four for a shilling. Well it was cheap. But meat, we never saw it. Vegetables: garden full. We never saw them. He wasn't growing for the house. He was growing for the show. Even his celery, it used to go to the show but it never come back. Same with his beetroot, it went to the show, it never come back. And it all went to the show but it never came back again. And that's why we were hungry. He sold it or gave it away. If you're taking maybe four lots of potatoes and you're taking maybe three or four lots of beetroot, in a small garden – I've seen my mother after my father went to bed at night, and then she would sneak out and take us some potatoes up. Maybe at eleven o'clock at night. But you couldn't blame her, because she was hungry as well. Everybody was hungry. My mother cried over the washing-tub and she was following the washing-tubs six days a week. Two and six a day. Up at morning. I'se crying, me mother's crying, all the others are crying, there wasn't a fire, there wasn't a bit of tea, there wasn't a bit of sugar, no nothing.

**Joe Bill Lightfoot,** quoted by Melvyn Bragg in *Speak for England*

Questions

1 What did children at this time wear instead of shoes?
2 Where did Joe get his short trousers from?
3 What is a 'shakky down'?
4 Where did the boys sleep?
5 How many girls were there in the family?
6 Where was the lavatory?
7 What was the main food they ate?
8 What fish did they eat?
9 Why couldn't they eat the vegetables from the garden?
10 What effect did all this have on their mother?

Discussion point

What impression do you get of Joe's father from this, and why?

# Money madness

Bread should be free,
shelter should be free,
fire should be free
to all and anybody, all and anybody, all over the world.

We must regain our sanity about money
before we start killing one another about it.
It's one thing or the other.

**D. H. Lawrence**


# Wages

The wages of work is cash.
The wages of cash is want more cash.
The wages of want more cash is vicious competition.
The wages of vicious competition is – the world we live in.

The work–cash–want circle is the viciousest circle
that ever turned men into fiends.

Earning a wage is a prison occupation
and a wage-earner is a sort of gaol-bird.

Earning a salary is a prison-overseer's job
a gaoler instead of a gaol-bird.

Living on our income is strolling grandly outside the prison
in terror lest you have to go in. And since the work-prison covers
almost every scrap of the living earth, you stroll up and down
on a narrow beat, about the same as a prisoner taking exercise.

This is called universal freedom.

**D. H. Lawrence**

# Song of the man who has money

I cannot but ask, in the park and the streets
When I look at the number of persons one meets,
What e'er in the world the poor devils can do
Whose fathers and mothers can't give them a *sou*.
    So needful it is to have money, heigh-ho!
    So needful it is to have money.

I ride, and I drive, and I care not a damn,
The people look up and they ask who I am;
And if I should chance to run over a cad,
I can pay for the damage, if ever so bad.
    So useful it is to have money, heigh-ho!
    So useful it is to have money.

It was but this winter I came up to town,
And already I'm gaining a sort of renown;
Find my way to good houses without much ado,
Am beginning to see the nobility too.
    So useful it is to have money, heigh-ho!
    So useful it is to have money.

O dear what a pity they ever should lose it,
Since they are the people who know how to use it;
So easy, so stately, such manners, such dinners,
And yet, after all, it is we are the winners.
    So needful it is to have money, heigh-ho!
    So needful it is to have money.

As for that, pass the bottle, and d____n the expense,
I've seen it observed by a writer of sense,
That labouring classes could scarce live a day,
If people like us didn't eat, drink, and pay.
    So useful it is to have money, heigh-ho!
    So useful it is to have money.

**Arthur Hugh Clough**

# *The people race*

*Problems of affluence in a community of rats.*

Our colony thrived and grew. We had plenty to eat, running water, electricity, a fan to draw in fresh air, a lift, a refrigerator. Deep underground, our home stayed warm in winter and cool in summer. It was a comfortable, almost luxurious existence.

And yet all was not well. After the first burst of energy, the moving in of the machines, the digging of tunnels and rooms, a feeling of discontent settled upon us like some creeping disease.

We were reluctant to admit it at first. We tried to ignore the feeling or to fight it off by building more things – bigger rooms, fancier furniture, carpeted hallways, things we did not really need. I was reminded of a story I had read. It was about a woman in a small town who bought a vacuum cleaner. Her name was Mrs Jones, and up until then she, like all of her neighbours, had kept her house spotlessly clean by using a broom and a mop. But the vacuum cleaner did it faster and better, and soon Mrs Jones was the envy of all the other housewives in town – so they bought vacuum cleaners, too.

The vacuum cleaner business was so brisk, in fact, that the company that made them opened a branch factory in the town. The factory used a lot of electricity, of course, and so did the women with their vacuum cleaners, so the local electric power company had to put up a new plant to keep them running. The power plant burned coal, and out of its chimneys black smoke poured blanketing the town with soot and making all the floors dirtier than ever. Still, by working twice as hard and twice as long, the women of the town were able to keep their floors *almost* as clean as they had been before Mrs Jones ever bought a vacuum cleaner in the first place.

The story was called 'The Rat Race' – which, I learned, means a race where, no matter how fast you run, you don't get anywhere. But there was nothing in the book about rats, and I felt bad about the title because, I thought, it wasn't a rat race at all, it was a People Race, and no sensible rats would ever do anything so foolish.

And yet here we were, rats getting caught up in something a lot like the People Race, and for no good reason. And the worst thing was that even with our make-work projects, we didn't really have enough to do.

**Robert O'Brien,** *Mrs Frisby and the Rats of NIMH*

# *Wealth*

Kino had found the Pearl of the World. In the town, in little offices, sat the men who bought pearls from the fishers. They waited in their chairs until the pearls came in and then they cackled and fought and shouted and threatened until they reached the lowest price the fishermen would stand. But there was a price below which they dared not go, for it had happened that a fisherman in despair had given his pearls to the church. And when the buying was over, these buyers sat alone and their fingers played restlessly with the pearls, and they wished they owned the pearls. For there were not many buyers really – there was only one, and he kept these agents in separate offices to give a semblance of competition. The news came to these men, and their eyes squinted and their fingertips burned a little, and each one thought how the patron could not live for ever and someone had to take his place. And each one thought how with some capital he could get a new start.

All manner of people grew interested in Kino – people with things to sell and people with favours to ask. Kino had found the Pearl of the World. Every man suddenly became related to Kino's pearl, and Kino's pearl went into the dreams, the speculations, the schemes, the plans, the futures, the wishes, the needs, the lusts, the hungers, of everyone, and only one person stood in the way and that was Kino, so that he became curiously every man's enemy.

But Kino and Juana did not know these things. Because they were happy and excited they thought everyone shared their joy. The house was crowded with neighbours. Kino held the great pearl in his hand, and it was warm and alive in his hand. And the music of the pearl had merged with the music of the family so that one beautified the other. The neighbours looked at the pearl in Kino's hand and they wondered how such luck could come to any man.

And Juan Tomás asked: 'What will you do now that you have become a rich man?'

Kino looked into his pearl, and Juana cast her eyelashes down and arranged her shawl to cover her face so that her excitement could not be seen. And in the incandescence of the pearl the pictures formed of the things Kino's mind had considered in the past and had given up as impossible. In the pearl he saw Juana and Coyotito and himself standing and kneeling at the high altar, and they were being married now that they could pay. He spoke softly: 'We will be married – in the church'.

In the pearl he saw how they were dressed – Juana in a shawl stiff with newness and a new skirt, and from under the long skirt Kino could see that she wore shoes. It was in the pearl – the picture glowing there. He himself was dressed in new white clothes, and he carried a new hat – not of straw but of fine black felt – and he too wore shoes – not sandals but shoes that laced. But Coyotito – he was the one – he wore a blue sailor suit and a little yachting cap.

And the music of the pearl rose like a chorus of trumpets in his ears.

Then to the lovely grey surface of the pearl came the little things Kino wanted: a harpoon to take the place of one lost a year ago, a new harpoon of iron with a ring in the end of the shaft; and – his mind could hardly make the leap – a rifle – but why not, since he was so rich? And Kino saw Kino in the pearl, Kino holding a Winchester carbine. It was the wildest daydreaming and very pleasant. His lips moved hesitantly over this. 'A rifle,' he said. 'Perhaps a rifle.'

It was the rifle that broke down the barriers. This was an impossibility, and if he could think of having a rifle whole horizons were burst and he could rush on. For it is said that humans are never satisfied, that you give them one thing and they want something more.

The neighbours, close pressed and silent in the house, nodded their heads at his wild imaginings. And a man in the rear murmured: 'A rifle. He will have a rifle.'

But the music of the pearl was shrilling with triumph in Kino. Juana looked up, and her eyes were wide at Kino's courage and at his imagination. And electric strength had come to him now the horizons were kicked out. In the pearl he saw Coyotito sitting at a little desk in a school, just as Kino had once seen it through an open door. And Coyotito was dressed in a jacket, and he had on a white collar and a broad silken tie. Moreover, Coyotito was writing on a big piece of paper. Kino looked at his neighbours fiercely. 'My son will go to school,' he said, and the neighbours were hushed. Juana caught her breath sharply. Her eyes were bright as she watched him, and she looked quickly down at Coyotito in her arms to see whether this might be possible.

But Kino's face shone with prophecy. 'My son will read and open the books, and my son will write and will know writing. And my son will make numbers, and these things will make us free because he will know – and through him we will know.' And in the pearl Kino saw himself and Juana squatting by the little fire in the brush hut while Coyotito read from a great book. 'This is what the pearl will do,' said Kino. And he had never said so many words together in his life. And suddenly he was afraid of his talking. His hand closed down over the pearl and cut the light away from it.

**John Steinbeck,** *The Pearl*

# The miser

Scrooge! a squeezing, wrenching, grasping, scraping, clutching, covetous old sinner! Hard and sharp as flint, from which no steel had ever struck out generous fire; secret, and self-contained, and solitary as an oyster. The cold within him froze his old features, nipped his pointed nose, shrivelled his cheek, stiffened his gait; made his eyes red, his thin lips blue; and spoke out shrewdly in his grating voice. A frosty rime was on his head, and on his eyebrows, and his wiry chin. He carried his own low temperature always about with him; he iced his office in the dog-days; and didn't thaw it one degree at Christmas.

External heat and cold had little influence on Scrooge. No warmth could warm, nor wintry weather chill him. No wind that blew was bitterer than he, no falling snow was more intent upon its purpose, no pelting rain less open to entreaty. Foul weather didn't know where to have him. The heaviest rain, and snow, and hail, and sleet, could boast of the advantage over him in only one respect. They often 'came down' handsomely, and Scrooge never did.

Nobody ever stopped him in the street to say, with gladsome looks, 'My dear Scrooge, how are you? when will you come to see me?' No beggars implored him to bestow a trifle, no children asked him what it was o'clock, no man or woman ever once in all his life inquired the way to such and such a place, of Scrooge.

But what did Scrooge care? It was the very thing he liked. To edge his way along the crowded paths of life, warning all human sympathy to keep its distance, was what the knowing ones call 'nuts' to Scrooge.

Once upon a time – of all the good days in the year, on Christmas Eve – old Scrooge sat busy in his counting-house. It was cold, bleak, biting weather: foggy withal: and he could hear the people in the court outside, go wheezing up and down, beating their hands upon their breasts, and stamping their feet upon the pavement-stones to warm them. The city clocks had only just gone three, but it was quite dark already: it had not been light all day: and candles were flaring in the windows of the neighbouring offices, like ruddy smears upon the palpable brown air. The fog came pouring in at every chink and keyhole, and was so dense without, that although the court was of the narrowest, the houses opposite were mere phantoms. To see the dingy cloud come drooping down, obscuring everything, one might have thought that Nature lived hard by, and was brewing on a large scale.

The door of Scrooge's counting-house was open that he might keep his eye upon his clerk, who in a dismal little cell beyond, a sort of tank, was copying letters. Scrooge had a very small fire, but the clerk's fire was so very much smaller that it looked like one coal. But he couldn't replenish it, for Scrooge kept the coal-box in his own room; and so surely as the clerk came in with the shovel, the master predicted that it would be necessary for them to part. Wherefore the clerk put on his white comforter, and tried to warm himself at the candle; in which effort, not being a man of a strong imagination, he failed.

'A merry Christmas, uncle! God save you!' cried a cheerful voice. It was the voice of Scrooge's nephew, who came upon him so quickly that this was the first intimation he had of his approach.

'Bah!' said Scrooge, 'Humbug!'

He had so heated himself with rapid walking in the fog and frost, this nephew of Scrooge's, that he was all in a glow; his face was ruddy and handsome; his eyes sparkled, and his breath smoked again.

'Christmas a humbug, uncle!' said Scrooge's nephew. 'You don't mean that, I am sure?'

'I do,' said Scrooge. 'Merry Christmas! What right have you to be merry? what reason have you to be merry? You're poor enough.'

'Come, then,' returned the nephew gaily. 'What right have you to be dismal? what reason have you to be morose? You're rich enough.'

Scrooge having no better answer ready on the spur of the moment said, 'Bah!' again; and followed it up with 'Humbug.'

'Don't be cross, uncle,' said the nephew.

'What else can I be,' returned the uncle, 'when I live in such a world of fools as this? Merry Christmas! Out upon merry Christmas! What's Christmas time to you but a time for paying bills without money; a time for finding yourself a year older, and not an hour richer; a time for balancing your books and having every item in 'em through a round dozen of months presented dead against you? If I could work my will,' said Scrooge, indignantly, 'every idiot who goes about with "Merry Christmas," on his lips, should be boiled with his own pudding, and buried with a stake of holly through his heart. He should!'

'Uncle!' pleaded the nephew.

'Nephew!' returned the uncle, sternly, 'keep Christmas in your own way, and let me keep it in mine.'

'Keep it!' repeated Scrooge's nephew. 'But you don't keep it.'

'Let me leave it alone, then,' said Scrooge. 'Much good may it do you! Much good it has ever done you!'

**Charles Dickens,** *A Christmas Carol*

# *The cost of living: 1938*

## What people earned

In 1938 the average industrial wage was £2/13/0 for a 53-hour week.
In 1950 the average industrial wage was £7/10/0 for a 46-hour week.
In 1980 the average wage for manual work was £113 for a 43-hour week.

# The cost of living: 1950

## Old money

The English currency was changed to its present form in 1971.
Before that the pound was divided into shillings and pence.

    £1  =  20 shillings (usually written 20/-)
    1/- =  12 pence (usually written 12d)

*Conversion:*

| old money | modern money | old money | modern money |
|-----------|--------------|-----------|--------------|
| 1d | £0.00·42 | 2/- | £0.10 |
| 2d | £0.00·8 | 2/6 | £0.12·5 |
| 6d | £0.02·5 | 5/- | £0.25 |
| 1/- | £0.05 | 10/- | £0.50 |

# *1950–1980*

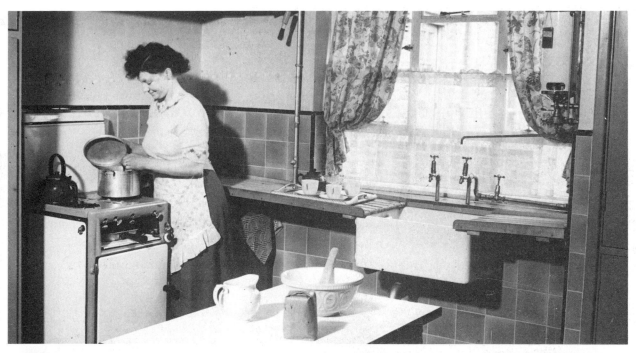

Questions   1   In 1938 a small saloon car cost £139. In 1980 a comparable car cost about £3,000. Compare the wages earned in 1938 and 1980. Which car was really more expensive and why?

2   In 1950 a chicken cost £1/10/0. In 1980 a similar chicken cost £3, exactly twice as much, in money terms. Compare wages for the two years. Which chicken actually cost more?

3   In 1980 the average weekly wage was about 15 times what it was in 1950, in money terms. Which of the things shown on page 84 do you think were really more expensive and which were cheaper in 1950 than 1980?

4   What are the main differences you can see between the two pictures on page 85? Comparing them, how do you think life changed between 1950 and 1980?

5   Look at the advertisements on pages 83 and 84. How do they compare with modern advertisements for similar things? Why do you think this is?

Research   1   Find modern advertisements for similar products to those advertised on pages 83 and 84. Compare the two sets of advertisements and write about the main differences you have observed.

2   Find out the price today of all the items listed on pages 83 and 84. How have these prices changed, *compared with each other*?

3   Find people who can remember what the cost of living was like in 1938 and in 1950. Show them the material on pages 83 and 84. Talk to them about what they remember life was like then. Write a report on what you find out.

Writing   1   It is the year 2015. Make up a page of advertisements about similar things to those shown on pages 83 and 84, but with 'up-to-date' details.

2   Write a survey for the year 2015 comparing life 'now' with what it was like 'back in the 1980s'.

# The Wedge-tailed Eagle

by Geoffrey Dutton

Through the hot, cloudless days in the back of New South Wales, there is always something beside the sun watching you from the sky. Over the line of the hills, or above the long stretches of plains, a black dot swings round and round; and its circles rise slowly or fall slowly, or simply remain at the same height, swinging in endless indolent curves, while the eyes watch the miles of earth below, and the six- or maybe nine-foot wingspan remains motionless in the air. You know that there is nothing you can do which will not be observed, that the circling eagle, however small the distance may make it, however aloof its flight may seem, has always fixed upon the earth an attention as fierce as its claws.

But the eagles watch the sky as well as the earth, and not only for other birds; when an Air Force station was established in their country in 1941, they were not alarmed by the noisy yellow aeroplanes. Occasionally they would even float in circles across the aerodrome itself, and then disappear again behind the hills; the pilots had little fear of colliding with one of these circling, watchful birds. The vast, brown-black shape of the eagle would appear before the little Tiger Moth biplane and then be gone. There was nothing more to it. No question of haste or flapping of wings, simply a flick over and down and then the eagle would resume its circling. Sometimes a pilot would chase the bird and would find, unexpectedly, no response; the eagle would seem not to notice the aeroplane and hold the course of its circling until the very moment when collision seemed inevitable. Then there would be the quick turn over, under, or away from the plane, with the great span of the wings unstirred.

The delay and the quick manœuvre would be done with a princely detachment and consciousness of superiority, the eagle in the silence of its wings scorning the roar and fuss of the aircraft and its engine.

Two pilots from the station were drinking one day in the local town with one of the farmers over whose land they used to fly.

'Two of us, you know, could do it,' one of them said. 'By yourself it's hopeless. The eagle can outfly you without moving his wings. But with two of you, one could chase him round while the other climbed above and dived at him. That way you'd at last get him flustered.'

The farmer was not at all hopeful.

'Maybe it'd take more than a couple of planes to fluster an eaglehawk. There's a big one around my place, just about twelve feet across. I wish you could get him. Though if you did hit him, there mightn't be much left of your little aeroplane.'

'It always beats me why you call them eaglehawks,' said one of the pilots. 'The wedge-tailed eagle is the biggest eagle in the world. You ought to pay him more respect, the most magnificent, majestic bird there is.'

The farmer was hostile to this idea of majesty.

'Have you ever seen them close-up? Or ever seen them feeding? The king of birds landing on a lolly-legged lamb and tearing him to bits. Or an old, dead, fly-blown ewe that's been fool enough to lie down with her legs uphill. Watch him hacking his way into their guts, with the vermin dancing all over his stinking brown feathers. Then all you've got to do is to let him see you five hundred yards off and up he flaps, slow and awkward, to a myall where he sits all bunched-up looking as if he's going to overbalance the little tree. Still, go ahead with your scheme. I'd like to see you beat one at his own game.'

He left, and the two others continued discussing their plans. A pilot in a small, aerobatic aircraft is like a child. He longs for something to play with. He can be happy enough, rolling and looping by himself in the sky, but happiness changes to a kind of ecstasy when there is someone against whom to match his skill, or someone to applaud him when he low-flies through the unforeseeable complications of tree and rock, hill and river. The contest becomes more wonderful the nearer it approaches death, when all else is forgotten in the concentration of the minute. The pilot who fights with bullets and shells is ecstatically involved in his action. This fight with the wedge-tailed eagle was to be to the death, not a battle of bullets or shells, but of skill against inborn mastery. The risk of death would be there, just the same, both for the bird and for the pilot supported by the fragile wood and fabric of the aeroplane.

One cloudless morning the pilots flew off together, in close formation, towards the valley of the farmer's house. The sky was as clean as a gun-barrel and the sun hit them both in the back of the neck as they flew westward towards the scrubby range and the

valley beyond. The pilot of the leading aircraft loosened his helmet
and let the wind, like a cool rushing sense of elation and freedom,
blow around his neck and hair. Like the eagle, he was a watcher, one
from whom no secrets could hide on the earth below. The country
matched the element in which he moved: both hard and unforgiving
of mistakes, yet endlessly stretching, magnificent in freedom.
Neither the air nor this land would bring anything for the asking;
but they would offer all manner of their peculiar riches to anyone
who could conquer them by work and vigilance and love. The
foolish and the weak perished like the sheep stuck in the wet mud of
the drying dams, in sight of the water for the lack of which they
died.

As he approached the hills, the earth below him and the creeks
were brown and dry as a walnut, with a strip of green along the
river and a few bright squares where a farmer had sunk a bore and
put in a few acres of lucerne. A mob of sheep stirred along in a cloud
of dust through a few scattered myalls and gum trees. He finally
bounced over the hills through air rough from the hot rocks, and
turning away from the other aeroplane, moved up the broad valley,
searching the sky for the black dot of an eagle wheeling and
wheeling like a windmill on its side. There was no sign of anything,
not even of a cloud or a high whirly of dust, which in an empty sky
looks like a patch of rust in a gun-barrel. Everything seemed to him
shiny and empty, yet somehow waiting to go off.

He made a long leisurely run up the valley, a few feet above the ground, lifting his wing over a fence or two, turning round a gum tree or away from a mob of sheep. The only other sign of life was the farmer standing near his truck by the gate of a paddock. He answered his wave, turned and flew over him, and then continued up the valley. Above him, in the other aeroplane, his friend waited for something to happen.

He ran his wheels almost along the ground and turned another fence. Suddenly the whole top of a tree flapped off in front of him and the eagle disappeared behind him before he could turn. Another bird rose from a dead sheep a few hundred yards away, but the pilot's attention was concentrated on the bird that had risen from the myall tree. It was undoubtedly the big eagle of which the farmer had told them.

By the time he had turned and come back in a climb the eagle was five hundred feet above him. He opened the throttle wide and pulled the strap of his helmet tight. He looked for the other plane and saw that his friend was moving towards them and climbing also, so that with the added height he could dive as they had planned.

The pilot was astonished to find that he was being out-climbed without the bird even moving a feather of its wings. On the hot, unseen currents it swung lazily round and round, its motionless wings always above the quivering, roaring aircraft. To make things worse, the pilot, in order to climb as quickly as possible, had to move in a straight line and then turn back, whereas the eagle sailed up in a close spiral. His hand pushed harder on the small knob of the throttle already wide open against the stop. Perhaps the battle would come to no more than this, the noisy pursuit of an enemy who could never be reached.

Yet the eagle, its mastery already established, now deliberately ceased climbing and waited for the aeroplane to struggle up to its level. The pilot, wondering if the farmer below had seen his humiliation, pressed on above the bird, where at about three thousand feet he levelled off and waved to his friend above that the battle was about to begin.

He came round in a curve at the bird, the aeroplane on the edge of stalling, juddering all over, the control-stick suddenly going limp in his hand as a pump-handle when a tank is dry, the slots on the end of the wings clattering above him; and then, just as he ducked his head to avoid the shining curved beak, the braced black and brown feathers, the sky amazingly was empty in front of him. The eagle had flicked over as lightly as a swallow, with no sign of panic or haste. He looked over and saw it below him, circling as quietly as if nothing in the whole morning, in the sky or on the land, had disturbed its watchful mastery of the air.

As the pilot dived towards it and followed it around again, he saw his friend drop his wing and come down, steep and straight to make the attack they had planned. He could see that the eagle, under its apparent negligence, was watching him and not the diving plane. This was the moment for which they had waited, when the eagle would break away as usual, but to find another aeroplane coming at it before it had time to move. The pilot's heart lunged inside him like the needle of the revolution counter on the instrument panel. Waiting until his friend had only another few hundred feet of his dive left, he jerked the controls hard over towards the shining feathers of the bird. It turned and fell below him, exactly as they had hoped it would. The pilot pulled himself up against his straps to watch its flight. The other aeroplane was on it just as it began its circling again. But the collision did not happen. The plane shot on and began to pull up out of its dive; the eagle recovered again into its slow swinging, a few hundred feet lower.

Yet it had shown a little concern. For the first time a fraction of dignity had been lost: momentarily the great wings had been disturbed a little from their full stretch. It had been startled into a quick defensive action. The pilot's excitement now blotted out everything but the battle in progress, leaving him poised between earth and sky, forgetful of both except as a blur of blue, a rush of brown. The last thing he saw on land had been the farmer's truck coming across the paddocks to a point somewhere below. Then all the vanity and pride in him had responded to the fact that there was someone to watch him. Now no response existed except to the detail of the black, polished brownness of the eagle's plumage, the glistening beak, the wedge-shaped tail. His excitement was at that intensity which is part of hope, his first sight of achievement. Previously the insolent negligence of the bird had destroyed his confidence, and had almost made the air feel the alien element it really was. In contrast with all his noisy manœuvring, his juggling with engine and controls, the eagle had scorned him with its silence, with its refusal to flap its wings, its mastery of the motionless sweep, the quick flick to safety and then the motionless circling again. The pilot had begun to wonder who was playing with whom. Perhaps the bird would suddenly turn, dive, rip him with a talon, and slide sideways down the vast slope to earth.

Yet now the eagle had been forced to move its wings, and he had seen the first sign of victory. Sweat poured round his helmet and down his neck and chest. His shirt clung wetly first to his flesh and then to the parachute harness. He looked at his altimeter and saw that they were down to seven hundred feet. Above him his friend was ready.

He turned in again towards the eagle. The aeroplane shivered
and clung to height, on the last fraction of speed before the spin.
Feeling the stiffness of his hands and feet on the controls, he told
himself to relax like the eagle in front of him. He looked quickly
upwards and saw his friend begin to dive. This was the second stage
of their plan. The eagle, however little sign of it appeared, knew
now that both aeroplanes were attacking. It circled, still on
unmoving wings, but subtler and harder to follow, and shifted
height slightly as it swung around.

The other plane was almost past him in its dive when he
completed his turn in a vicious swing towards the eagle; he missed,
spun, corrected, looked up to see the other aeroplane, which had
dived this time far below the eagle, coming almost vertically up
below the just-levelled bird.

The eagle heard and saw, and flicked over to where, before,
safety had always been emptily waiting for it. It flashed, wings still
gloriously outstretched, straight into the right-hand end of the
upper mainplane of the aircraft, exactly where the metal slot curves
across the wood and fabric. Its right wing, at the point where the
hard, long feathers give way to the soft, curved feathers of the body,
snapped away and fluttered down to earth. The left wing folded into
the body, stretched and folded again, as the heavy box of bone, beak
and claw plunged and slewed to the ground. The pilot could not
watch the last few feet of its descent. For the first time he was
grateful to the roar of the motor that obscured the thud of the body
striking earth.

The two pilots landed in the paddock, and, leaving the engines running, walked over to the dark mass of feathers. One of them turned off to the side and came back holding the severed wing. It was almost as big as the man himself.

The two of them stood in silence. The moment of skill and danger was past, and the dead body before them proclaimed their victory. Frowning with the glare of the sun and the misery of their achievement they both looked down at the piteous, one-winged eagle. Not a mark of blood was on it, the beak glistening and uncrushed, the ribbed feet and talons clenched together. It was not the fact of death that kept them in silence; the watcher could not always keep his station in the air. What both of them could still see was the one-winged heap of bone and feathers, slewing and jerking uncontrolled to earth.

In the distance they heard the noise of the farmer's truck approaching, and saw it stop at a gate and the farmer wave as he got out to open it. They quickly picked up the bird and its wing, and ran with them to the little hillock covered in rocks at the corner of the paddock. Between two large rocks they folded both wings across the bird and piled stones above it; and then, each lifting, carried a large flat stone and placed it above the others.

As they ran back towards the aeroplane a black dot broke from the hills and swung out above them, circling round and round, watching the truck accelerate and then stop as the two aeroplanes turned, taxied and slid into the air before it could reach them.

| | |
|---|---|
| Questions to think and talk about | Page 87  What impression do you get of the eagle from this page? |
| | Page 88  What do you learn here about the eagle's flying skill? |
| | Page 89  What is the pilots' opinion of the eagle? |
| | What is the farmer's opinion of it? |
| | Page 90  How did the pilot feel as he searched? |
| | Page 91  Who was the better flier – the eagle or the pilot in his plane? |
| | Pages 92 and 93  What were the pilots trying to do? |
| | Page 94  How was the eagle killed? |
| | Page 95  Why did the pilots bury the eagle and then hurry away? |

**Discussion points**

What made the pilots want to kill the eagle?
How did they feel about its death at the end of the story?
What do you think of what they did?
Is it ever right to kill animals for sport?
Are there other ways in which men and animals can come together for sport, without cruelty?

**Writing**

Write a short story about a contest between a man and an animal. Either choose your own subject matter, or base your story on this photograph.

Write a short story that ends with these words:

. . . and even though I won in the end, I wondered if it had all been worthwhile.

# FUTURE IMPERFECT

These two stills are from films about the future.
What would life have been like in each of these future societies?
If you were making a film about life in the future, what would you
concentrate on?

Still from *Things To Come*, 1936

Still from *Metropolis*, 1926

# The examination

At five minutes to eleven, they called the name of Jordan.

'Good luck, son, his father said, without looking at him. 'I'll call for you when the test is over.'

Dickie walked to the door and turned the handle. The room inside was dim, and he could hardly make out the features of the grey-tunicked attendant who greeted him.

'Sit down,' the man said softly. He indicated a high stool beside his desk. 'Your name's Richard Jordan?'

'Yes, sir.'

'Your classification number is 600-115. Drink this, Richard.'

He lifted a plastic cup from the desk and handed it to the boy. The liquid inside it had the consistency of buttermilk and tasted vaguely of peppermint. Dickie downed it, and handed the man the empty cup.

He sat in silence, feeling drowsy, while the man wrote busily on a sheet of paper. Then the attendant looked at his watch, and rose to stand only inches from Dickie's face. He unclipped a penlike object from the pocket of his tunic and flashed a tiny light into the boy's eyes.

'All right,' he said. 'Come with me, Richard.'

He led Dickie to the end of the room, where a single wooden armchair faced a multi-dialled computing machine. There was a microphone on the left arm of the chair, and when the boy sat down, he found its pinpoint head conveniently at his mouth.

'Now just relax, Richard. You'll be asked some questions, and you think them over carefully. Then give your answers into the microphone. The machine will take care of the rest.'

'Yes, sir.'

'I'll leave you alone now. Whenever you want to start, just say "ready" into the microphone.'

'Yes, sir.'

The man squeezed his shoulder, and left.

Dickie said, 'Ready.'

Lights appeared on the machine, and a mechanism whirred. A voice said:

'Complete this sequence. One, four, seven, ten . . .'

\* \* \* \* \* \* \* \* \* \* \* \* \* \* \* \* \* \* \* \* \* \* \* \* \* \* \*

Mr and Mrs Jordan were in the living room, not speaking, not even speculating.

It was almost four o'clock when the telephone rang. The woman tried to reach it first, but her husband was quicker.

'Mr Jordan?'

The voice was clipped; a brisk, official voice.

'Yes, speaking.'

'This is the Government Educational Service. Your son, Richard M. Jordan, Classification 600-115, has completed the Government examination. We regret to inform you that his intelligence quotient has exceeded the Government regulation, according to Rule 84, Section 5, of the New Code.'

Across the room, the woman cried out, knowing nothing except the emotion she read on her husband's face.

'You may specify by telephone,' the voice droned on, 'whether you wish his body interred by the Government or would you prefer a private burial place? The fee for Government burial is ten dollars.'

**Henry Slesar,** *Examination Day*

| Questions to think and talk about | |
|---|---|
| | 1 What has happened to Dickie? |
| | 2 Why? |
| | 3 What do you think Rule 84 Section 5 of the New Code says? |
| | 4 Why should a Government make rules like that? |
| | 5 How do you think their society is organized? |
| | 6 What is the place in society of people like Dickie's parents? |
| | 7 Is there anything in the modern world to make you think that this could ever happen? |

Writing   The row of asterisks (*   *   *) shows that something has been missed out. Read the story carefully and imagine what happens between the two parts of the story. Think how much of it the writer would need to tell, in order to make the story complete. (For example, Dickie's father says, 'I'll call for you when the test is over.' Obviously he doesn't. Why not?) Then write the missing part of the story.

# To see the rabbit

We are going to see the rabbit.
We are going to see the rabbit.
Which rabbit, people say?
Which rabbit, ask the children?
Which rabbit?
The only rabbit,
The only rabbit in England,
Sitting behind a barbed-wire fence
Under the floodlights, neon lights,
10 Sodium lights,
Nibbling grass
On the only patch of grass
In England, in England
(Except the grass by the hoardings
Which doesn't count).
We are going to see the rabbit
And we must be there on time.
First we shall go by escalator,
Then we shall go by underground,
20 And then we shall go by motorway,
And then by helicopterway,
And the last ten yards we shall have to go
On foot.

And now we are going
All the way to see the rabbit,
We are nearly there,
We are longing to see it,
And so is the crowd
Which is here in thousands
30 With mounted policemen
And big loudspeakers
And bands and banners,
And everyone has come a long way.
But soon we shall see it
Sitting and nibbling
The blades of grass
On the only patch of grass
In – but something has gone wrong!
Why is everyone so angry,

40    Why is everyone jostling
And slanging and complaining?

The rabbit has gone,
Yes, the rabbit has gone.
He has actually burrowed down into the earth
And made himself a warren, under the earth,
Despite all these people.
And what shall we do?
What *can* we do?

It is all a pity, you must be disappointed,
50    Go home and do something else for today,
Go home again, go home for today.
For you cannot hear the rabbit, under the earth,
Remarking rather sadly to himself, by himself,
As he rests in his warren, under the earth:
'It won't be long, they are bound to come,
They are bound to come and find me, even here.'

**Alan Brownjohn**

**Questions**    1   Lines 1–23 describe some of the changes that have taken place between now and the time when the poem takes place. What are they?

2   How can you tell from lines 24–41 that going to see the rabbit is very popular?

3   How does the rabbit feel about it? How do you know?

4   What is the meaning of the last two lines?

5   What is Alan Brownjohn telling us in this poem?

6   Do you agree with him? What are your reasons?

**Writing**    You are Her Majesty's Keeper of The Rabbit. The strange disappearance of The Rabbit has caused a lot of anger in the Government and among the people. You are required to give an explanation and outline what you plan to do about it. Write your report.

# *Ageless?*

The year was 2158 A.D. and Lou and Emerald Schwartz were whispering on the balcony outside of Lou's family's apartment on the 76th floor of Building 257 in Alden Village, a New York housing development that covered what has once been known as Southern C Connecticut. When Lou and Emerald had married, Em's parents had tearfully described the marriage as being between May and December; but now, with Lou 112 and Em 93, Em's parents had to admit that the match had worked out surprisingly well.

But Em and Lou weren't without their troubles, and they were out in the nippy air of the balcony because of them. What they were saying was bitter and private.

'Sometimes I get so mad, I feel like just up and diluting his anti-gerasone,' said Em.

'That'd be against Nature, Em,' said Lou, 'it'd be murder. Besides, if he caught us tinkering with his anti-gerasone, not only would he disinherit us, he'd bust my neck. Just because he's 172 doesn't mean Gramps isn't as strong as a bull.'

'Against Nature,' said Em. 'Who knows what Nature's like any more? Ohhhhh – I don't guess I could ever bring myself to dilute his anti-gerasone or anything like that, but, gosh, Lou, a body can't help thinking Gramps is never going to leave if somebody doesn't help him along a little. Golly – we're so crowded a person can hardly turn around, and Verna's dying for a baby, and Melissa's gone thirty years without one.' She stamped her feet. 'I get so sick of seeing his wrinkled old face, watching him take the only private room and the best chair and the best food, and getting to pick out what to watch on TV, and running everybody's life by changing his will all the time.'

'Well, after all,' said Lou bleakly, 'Gramps *is* head of the family. And he can't help being wrinkled like he is. He was 70 before anti-gerasone was invented. He's going to leave, Em. Just give him time. It's his business. I know he's tough to live with, but be patient. It wouldn't do to do anything that'd rile him.'

'When *is* he going to leave, Lou?' said Emerald.

'Well, he's talking about giving up anti-gerasone right after the 500-mile Speedway Race.'

'Yes – and before that it was the Olympics, and before that the World's Series, and before that the Presidential Elections, and before that I-don't-know-what. It's been just one excuse after another for fifty years now. I don't think we're ever going to get a room to ourselves.'

'All right – call me a failure!' said Lou. 'What can I do? I work hard and make good money, but the whole thing practically is taxed away for defence and old-age pensions.'

Em put her arms around his neck. 'Lou, hon, I'm not calling you a failure. The Lord knows you're not. You just haven't had a chance to be anything or have anything because Gramps and the rest of his generation won't leave and let somebody else take over.'

'Yeah, yeah,' said Lou gloomily. 'You can't exactly blame 'em, though, can you? I mean, I wonder how quick we'll knock off the anti-gerasone when we get Gramps' age.'

'Sometimes I wish there wasn't any such thing as anti-gerasone!' said Emerald passionately. 'Or I wish it was made out of something real expensive and hard-to-get instead of mud and dandelions. Sometimes I wish folks just up and died regular as clockwork, without anything to say about it, instead of deciding themselves how long they're going to stay around. There ought to be a law against selling the stuff to anybody over a hundred and fifty.'

**Kurt Vonnegut,** *Tomorrow and Tomorrow and Tomorrow*

---

# Life in the twenty-first century

*In* News from Nowhere *(1888) William Morris described life in England in the twenty-first century. He imagined that a great socialist revolution had taken place in 1952. Money had been abolished and a society developed in which all men shared everything. The story is told by a visitor from the nineteenth century who finds himself in Kensington, but it is a very different Kensington from the city area he remembers.*

The road plunged at once into a beautiful wood spreading out on either side, but obviously much further on the north side, where even the oaks and sweet chestnuts were of a good growth; while the quicker-growing trees (amongst which I thought the planes and sycamores too numerous) were very big and fine-grown.

We came on many groups both coming and going, or wandering in the edges of the wood. Amongst these were many children from six or eight years old up to sixteen or seventeen. They seemed to me to be especially fine specimens of their race, and were clearly enjoying themselves to the utmost; some of them were hanging about little tents pitched on the greensward, and by some of these fires were burning, with pots hanging over them gipsy fashion. I said:

'Well, the youngsters here will be all the fresher for school when the summer gets over and they have to go back again.'

'School?' he said; 'yes, what do you mean by that word? I don't see how it can have anything to do with children. We talk, indeed, of a school of herring, and a school of painting, and in the former sense we might talk of a school of children – but otherwise,' said he laughing, 'I must own myself beaten.'

I thought I had best say nothing about the boy-farms which I had been used to call schools, as I saw pretty clearly that they had disappeared; and so I said after a little fumbling, 'I was using the word in the sense of a system of education.'

'Education?'

'Well, education means a system of teaching young people.'

'Why not old people also?' said he with a twinkle in his eye. 'But,' he went on, 'I can assure you our children learn, whether they go through a "system of teaching" or not. Why, you will not find one of these children about here, boy or girl, who cannot swim, and every one of them has been used to tumbling about the little forest ponies – there's one of them now! They all of them know how to cook; the bigger lads can mow; many can thatch and do odd jobs at carpentering; or they know how to keep shop. I can tell you they know plenty of things.'

'Yes, but their mental education, the teaching of their minds,' said I.

'Guest,' said he, 'perhaps you have not learned to do these things I have been speaking about; and if that's the case, don't you run away with the idea that it doesn't take some skill to do them, and doesn't give plenty of work for one's mind. But, however, I understand you to be speaking of book-learning; and as to that, it is a simple affair. Most children, seeing books lying about, manage to read by the time they are four years old; though I am told it has not always been so. As to writing, we do not encourage them to scrawl too early (though scrawl a little they will), because it gets them into a habit of ugly writing; and what's the use of a lot of ugly writing being done, when rough printing can be done so easily?'

'Well,' said I, 'about the children; when they know how to read and write, don't they learn something else – languages, for instance?'

'Of course,' he said; 'sometimes even before they can read, they can talk French, which is the nearest language talked on the other side of the water; and they soon get to know German also, which is talked by a huge number of communes and colleges on the

mainland. Children pick them up very quickly, because their elders all know them; and besides our guests from oversea often bring their children with them, and the little ones get together, and rub their speech into one another.'

'Well,' said I, 'what else do they learn? I suppose they don't all learn history?'

'No, no,' said he; 'some don't care about it; in fact, I don't think many do. I have heard my great-grandfather say that it is mostly in periods of turmoil and strife and confusion that people care much about history; and you know,' said my friend, with an amiable smile, 'we are not like that now. We don't encourage early bookishness, though you will find some children who *will* take to books very early; which perhaps is not good for them. We find that children are mostly given to imitating their elders, and when they see most people about them engaged in genuinely amusing work, like house-building and street paving, and gardening, and the like, that is what they want to be doing; so I don't think we need fear having too many book-learned men.'

'Yes,' said I, 'but suppose the child never wants the information, never grows in the direction you might hope him to do: suppose, for instance, he objects to learning arithmetic or mathematics; you can't force him when he *is* grown; can't you force him while he is growing, and oughtn't you to do so?'

'Well,' said he, 'were you forced to learn arithmetic and mathematics?'

'A little,' said I.

'And how old are you now?'

'Say fifty-six,' said I.

'And how much arithmetic and mathematics do you know now?' quoth the old man, smiling rather mockingly.

Said I: 'None whatever, I am sorry to say.'

Hammond laughed quietly, but made no other comment on my admission, and I dropped the subject of education, perceiving him to be hopeless on that side.

*The visitor and his guide find themselves in an area of small shops, or 'booths'.*

'Well,' said he, pleasantly, 'you may as well see what the inside of these booths is like: think of something you want.'

Said I: 'Could I get some tobacco and a pipe?'

'Of course,' said he; 'what was I thinking of, not asking you before? Well, Bob is always telling me that we non-smokers are a selfish lot, and I'm afraid he is right. But come along; here is a place just handy.'

Within were a couple of children – a brown skinned boy of

about twelve, who sat reading a book, and a pretty little girl of about a year older, who was sitting also reading behind the counter; they were obviously brother and sister.

'Good morning, little neighbours,' said Dick. 'My friend here wants tobacco and a pipe; can you help him?'

'O yes, certainly,' said the girl, 'what tobacco is it you would like?'

'Latakia,' quoth I, feeling as if I were assisting at a child's game, and wondering whether I should get any thing but make-believe.

But the girl took a dainty little basket from a shelf beside her, went to a jar, and took out a lot of tobacco and put the filled basket down on the counter before me, where I could both smell and see that it was excellent Latakia.

'But you haven't weighed it,' said I, 'and – and how much am I to take?'

'Why,' she said. 'I advise you to cram your bag, because you may be going where you can't get Latakia. Now for the pipe: that also you must let me choose for you; there are three pretty ones just come in.'

She disappeared again, and came back with a big-bowled pipe in her hand, carved out of some hard wood very elaborately, and mounted in gold sprinkled with little gems. It was, in short, as pretty and gay a toy as I had ever seen; something like the best kind of Japanese work, but better.

'Dear me!' said I, when I set eyes on it, 'this is altogether too grand for me, or for anybody but the Emperor of the World. Besides, I shall lose it: I always lose my pipes.'

The child seemed rather dashed, and said, 'Don't you like it, neighbour?'

'O yes,' I said, 'of course I like it.'

'Well, then, take it,' said she, 'and don't trouble about losing it. What will it matter if you do? Somebody is sure to find it, and he will use it, and you can get another.'

I took it out of her hand to look at it, and while I did so, forgot my caution, and said, 'But however am I to pay for such a thing as this?'

Dick laid his hand on my shoulder as I spoke, and turning I met his eyes with a comical expression in them, which warned me against another exhibition of extinct commercial morality; so I reddened and held my tongue, while the girl simply looked at me with the deepest gravity, as if I were a foreigner blundering in my speech, for she clearly didn't understand me a bit.

**William Morris,** *News from Nowhere*

# *The pedestrian*

To enter out into that silence that was the city at eight o'clock of a misty evening in November, to put your feet upon that buckling concrete walk, to step over grassy seams and make your way, hands in pockets, through the silences, that was what Mr Leonard Mead most dearly loved to do. He would stand upon the corner of an intersection and peer down long moonlit avenues of sidewalk in four directions, deciding which way to go, but it really made no difference; he was alone in this world of A.D. 2053, or as good as alone, and with a final decision made, a path selected, he would stride off, sending patterns of frosty air before him like the smoke of a cigar.

Sometimes he would walk for hours and miles and return only at midnight to his house. And on his way he would see the cottages and homes with their dark windows, and it was not unlike walking through a graveyard where only the faintest glimmers of firefly light appeared in flickers behind the windows. Sudden grey phantoms seemed to manifest upon inner room walls where a curtain was still undrawn against the night, or there were whisperings and murmurs where a window in a tomblike building was still open.

Mr Leonard Mead would pause, cock his head, listen, look, and march on, his feet making no noise on the lumpy walk. For long ago he had wisely changed to sneakers when strolling at night, because the dogs in intermittent squads would parallel his journey with barkings if he wore hard heels, and lights might click on and faces appear and an entire street be startled by the passing of a lone figure, himself, in the early November evening.

On this particular evening he began his journey in a westerly direction, towards the hidden sea. There was a good crystal frost in the air; it cut the nose and made the lungs blaze like a Christmas tree inside; you could feel the cold light going on and off, all the branches filled with invisible snow. He listened to the faint push of his soft shoes through autumn leaves with satisfaction, and whistled a cold quiet whistle between his teeth, occasionally picking up a leaf as he passed, examining its skeletal pattern in the infrequent lamplights as he went on, smelling its rusty smell.

'Hello, in there,' he whispered to every house on every side as he moved. 'What's up tonight on Channel 4, Channel 7, Channel 9? Where are the cowboys rushing, and do I see the United States Cavalry over the next hill to the rescue?'

The street was silent and long and empty, with only his shadow moving like the shadow of a hawk in mid-country. If he closed his eyes and stood very still, frozen, he could imagine himself upon the centre of a plain, a wintry, windless Arizona desert with no house in a thousand miles, and only dry river beds, the streets, for company.

'What is it now?' he asked the houses, noticing his wrist-watch. 'Eight-thirty p.m.? Time for a dozen assorted murders? A quiz? A revue? A comedian falling off the stage?'

Was that a murmur of laughter from within a moon-white house? He hesitated, but went on when nothing more happened. He stumbled over a particularly uneven section of sidewalk. The cement was vanishing under flowers and grass. In ten years of walking by night or day, for thousands of miles, he had never met another person walking, not one in all that time.

He came to a cloverleaf intersection which stood silent where two main highways crossed the town. During the day it was a thunderous surge of cars, the gas stations open, a great insect rustling and a ceaseless jockeying for position as the scarab-beetles, a faint incense puttering from their exhausts, skimmed homeward to the far directions. But now these highways, too, were like streams in a dry season, all stone and bed and moon radiance.

He turned back on a side street, circling around towards his home. He was within a block of his destination when the lone car turned a corner quite suddenly and flashed a fierce white cone of light upon him. He stood entranced, not unlike a night moth, stunned by the illumination, and then drawn towards it.

A metallic voice called to him:

'Stand still. Stay where you are! Don't move!'

He halted.

'Put up your hands!'

'But——' he said.

'Your hands up! Or we'll shoot!'

The police, of course, but what a rare, incredible thing; in a city of three million, there was only *one* police car left, wasn't that correct? Ever since a year ago, 2052, the election year, the force had been cut down from three cars to one. Crime was ebbing; there was no need now for the police, save for this one lone car wandering and wandering the empty streets.

'Your name?' said the police car in a metallic whisper. He couldn't see the men in it for the bright light in his eyes.

'Leonard Mead,' he said.

'Speak up!'

'Leonard Mead!'

'Business or profession?'

'I guess you'd call me a writer.'

'No profession,' said the police car, as if talking to itself. The light held him fixed, like a museum specimen, needle thrust through chest.

'You might say that,' said Mr Mead. He hadn't written in years. Magazines and books didn't sell any more. Everything went on in the tomblike houses at night now, he thought, continuing his fancy. The tombs, ill-lit by television light, where the people sat like the dead, the grey or multicoloured lights touching their faces, but never really touching *them*.

'No profession,' said the phonograph voice, hissing. 'What are you doing out?'

'Walking,' said Leonard Mead.

'Walking!'

'Just walking,' he said simply, but his face felt cold.

'Walking, just walking, walking?'

'Yes, sir.'

'Walking where? For what?'

'Walking for air. Walking to *see*.'

'Your address!'

'Eleven South Saint James Street.'

'And there is air *in* your house, you have an air *conditioner*, Mr Mead?'

'Yes.'

'And you have a viewing screen in your house to see with?'

'No.'

'No?' There was a crackling quiet that in itself was an accusation.

'Are you married, Mr Mead?'

'No.'

'Not married,' said the police voice behind the fiery beam. The moon was high and clear among the stars and the houses were grey and silent.

'Nobody wanted me,' said Leonard Mead with a smile.

'Don't speak unless you're spoken to!'

Leonard Mead waited in the cold night.

'Just *walking*, Mr Mead?'

'Yes.'

'But you haven't explained for what purpose.'

'I explained; for air, and to see, and just to walk.'

'Have you done this often?'

'Every night for years.'

The police car sat in the centre of the street with its radio throat faintly humming.

'Well, Mr Mead,' it said.

'Is that all?' he asked politely.

'Yes,' said the voice. 'Here.' There was a sigh, a pop. The back door of the police car sprang wide. 'Get in.'

'Wait a minute, I haven't done anything!'

'Get in.'

'I protest!'

'Mr Mead.'

He walked like a man suddenly drunk. As he passed the front window of the car he looked in. As he had expected, there was no one in the front seat, no one in the car at all.

'Get in.'

He put his hand to the door and peered into the back seat, which was a little cell, a little black jail with bars. It smelled of riveted steel. It smelled of harsh antiseptic; it smelled too clean and hard and metallic. There was nothing soft there.

'Now if you had a wife to give you an alibi,' said the iron voice. 'But——'

'Where are you taking me?'

The car hesitated, or rather gave a faint whirring click, as if information, somewhere, was dripping card by punch-slotted card under electric eyes. 'To the Psychiatric Centre for Research on Regressive Tendencies.'

He got in. The door shut with a soft thud. The police car rolled through the night avenues, flashing its dim lights ahead.

They passed one house on one street a moment later, one house in an entire city of houses that were dark, but this one particular house had all of its electric lights brightly lit, every window a loud yellow illumination, square and warm in the cool darkness.

'That's *my* house,' said Leonard Mead.

No one answered him.

The car moved down the empty river-bed streets and off away, leaving the empty streets with the empty sidewalks, and no sound and no motion all the rest of the chill November night.

**Ray Bradbury**

# The knowledge explosion

Imagine a clock face with sixty minutes on it. Let the clock stand for the time men have had access to writing systems. Our clock would thus represent something like three thousand years, and each minute on our clock fifty years. On this scale, there were no significant media changes until about nine minutes ago. At that time, the printing press came into use. About three minutes ago, the telegraph, photograph, and locomotive arrived. Two minutes ago: the telephone, rotary press, motion pictures, automobile, aeroplane and radio. One minute ago, the talking picture. Television has appeared in the last ten seconds, the computer in the last five, and communications satellites in the last second. The laser beam appeared only a fraction of a second ago.

It would be possible to place almost any area of life on our clock face and get roughly the same measurements. For example, in medicine, you would have almost no significant changes until about one minute ago. About a minute ago antibiotics arrived. About ten seconds ago, open-heart surgery. In fact, within the past ten seconds there probably have been more changes in medicine than is represented by all the rest of the time on our clock. This is what some people call the 'knowledge explosion'.

Of course, this state of affairs applies to our education as well. If you are over twenty-five years of age, the mathematics you were taught in school is 'old'; the grammar you were taught is obsolete and in disrepute; the biology completely out of date, and history open to serious question. The best that can be said of you, assuming that you *remember* most of what you were told and read, is that you are a walking encyclopaedia of outdated information.

**Postman and Weingartner,** *Teaching as a Subversive Activity (1969)*

**Questions**

1   Copy and complete this chart:

| 'minutes'/'seconds' ago | discoveries/inventions |
|---|---|
| 9 minutes | printing |
| 3 minutes | telegraph, photography . . . |

2   Write a short explanation of what is meant by the 'knowledge explosion'.

**Research**   Find out just how different your education is from that your parents received. Write a description of the main changes that have taken place.

# Thinking and writing about the unit

**1**   Most of the writers in this unit have chosen one aspect of life *now* as the basis of their look at the future. Kurt Vonnegut for example, takes the increasing average age of the population. What do *you* think is the most serious problem facing us? How will it develop in the future?

*Either*   write detailed answers to these questions;
*or*   write a story about the future based on your answers.

**2**   The unit is called *Future Imperfect*. It takes a fairly gloomy view of the future. Is it right to do this? What are the good things we should be looking forward to? What can be done to avoid the bad ones?

*Either*   write detailed answers to these questions;
*or*   write a story about the future in which everything has got better and men live in an ideal, perfect society.

**3**   Time has moved on about twenty-five years. It is your fortieth birthday. You have a son or daughter who is the age that you are now. You look back on your life and you tell your son or daughter about the changes that you have seen and how you feel about those changes.

Write the conversation that takes place between the two of you.

# BLUE HORIZONS

1

2    These are both pictures of Palermo, Sicily.

113

# Two views of Morocco

The incredibly beautiful country of Morocco is the most distant outpost of Islam, separated from the rest of Africa by the rugged Atlas Mountains and the waterless wastes of the Sahara. The mountains and plains are the home of the Berber, a fiercely independent people who've kept their way of life despite many intrusions; in the desert are nomadic Blue Men whose skin is tinged with the dye from their indigo robes. Morocco is a land of vivid contrasts, with pale, sandy beaches and deep blue seas; snow-capped mountains and green valleys; cedar forests and palm groves; tropical gardens and sunbaked deserts; whitewashed towns and red-mud fortresses; the historic imperial cities of Fez, Meknes, Rabat and Marrakesh, with their fascinating walled medinas side by side with the 'new' cities built by the French; and of course, the picturesque Mediterranean/Atlantic city of Tangier, traditional gateway to North Africa.

*Thomson Holidays brochure* (1980)

All people who work with their hands are partly invisible, and the more important the work they do, the less visible they are. Still, a white skin is always fairly conspicuous. In northern Europe, when you see a labourer ploughing a field, you probably give him a second glance. In a hot country, the chances are that you won't even see him. In a tropical landscape one's eye takes in everything except the human beings. It takes in the dried-up soil, the prickly pear, the palm tree and the distant mountain, but it always misses the peasant hoeing at his patch. He is the same colour as the earth, and a great deal less interesting to look at.

It is only because of this that the starved countries of Asia and Africa are accepted as tourist resorts. Where the human beings have brown skins their poverty is simply not noticed. What does Morocco mean to an Englishman? Camels, castles, palm trees, Foreign Legionnaires, brass trays and bandits. One could probably live there for years without noticing that for nine-tenths of the people the reality of life is an endless, back-breaking struggle to wring a little food out of an eroded soil.

Most of Morocco is so desolate that no wild animal bigger than a hare can live in it. Huge areas which were once covered with forest have turned into a treeless waste where the soil is exactly like broken-up brick. Nevertheless a good deal of it is cultivated, with frightful labour. Everything is done by hand. Long lines of women, bent double like inverted capital L's work their way slowly across the fields tearing up the prickly weeds with their hands, and the peasant gathering lucerne for fodder pulls it up stalk by stalk instead of reaping it, thus saving an inch or two on each stalk. The plough is a wretched wooden thing, so frail that one can easily carry it on one's shoulder, and fitted underneath with a rough iron spike which 30 stirs the soil to a depth of about four inches. This is as much as the strength of the animals is equal to.

Every afternoon a file of very old women passes down the road outside my house, each carrying a load of firewood. All of them are mummified with age and the sun, and all of them are tiny. But what is strange about these people is their invisibility. For several weeks, always at about the same time of day the file of old women had hobbled past the house with their firewood, and though they had registered themselves on my eyeballs I cannot truly say that I had seen them. Firewood was passing – and that was how I saw it. It was 40 only that one day I happened to be walking behind them, and the curious up-and-down motion of a load of wood drew my attention to the human being beneath it. Then for the first time I noticed the poor old earth-coloured bodies, bodies reduced to bones and leathery skin, bent double under the crushing weight. Yet I suppose I had not been five minutes on Moroccan soil before I noticed the overloading of the donkeys and was infuriated by it. Anyone can be sorry for the donkey with its galled back, but it is generally owing to some kind of accident if one even notices the old woman under her load of sticks.

**George Orwell,** *England, Your England* (1939)

| Questions to think and talk about | 1 What would George Orwell have thought about the first piece of writing? |
| --- | --- |

Questions to think and talk about
1 What would George Orwell have thought about the first piece of writing?
2 Orwell's main message is contained in his second paragraph. Do you think his argument is still true?
3 What effect does reading the two pieces have on you?

Writing
Choose a place that *either* you know very well *or* have visited as a tourist. Write two descriptions of it:
a in the style of a tourist brochure;
b as written by someone who has lived there for many years.

# *Rainbow*

We seemed to come upon the slum street rather unexpectedly, for it was tucked away behind a main thoroughfare known as Deansgate. It was an oddly quiet and deserted street, a single row of cottages that looked older and even more shabby than Back Cannon Street. There were no children playing nor the sound of voices. Broken windows had been patched up by old sacks. There was no pavement, the cobblestoned street area running right up to the front doors, which had no doorsteps. Down the middle of the narrow roadway ran a wet and smelly gutter. There were three or four old handcarts around, some tilted up against the houses, and one standing up in the roadway, which seemed to indicate that some inhabitants were rag-and-bone men or perhaps hawkers. There was a big cat waiting near a hole in a wall, as though expecting a rat or something. Seated at one open door were a small boy and girl quietly playing a game known as Jacks and Bobbers. They were bouncing a large marble known as a bobber, and in between picking up small cubes known as jacks. When they saw us standing there they looked uneasy, stopped playing and stood up.

'Slum kids,' whispered Ben. 'Look at 'em. Poor little things.'

'It's a shame,' said Sam. 'Summat should be done about it.'

Ben whispered out of the corner of his mouth – he was rather good at it: 'They shouldn't be allowed. Slum folk y'know. 'Avin' families an' that. That's what my Dad says.' Ben spread his feet apart in a comfortable stance and surveyed the scene and in particular the two small children. 'What good will they ever be to anybody?' he remarked. At times Ben could look quite brainy, and he did just then.

Then suddenly and unexpectedly a girl emerged from behind the big handcart that had been standing in the street. She was wearing a flimsy dress, and had sturdy legs and bare feet. She was quite striking in some way, for she had thick curly black hair and dark blue eyes and held herself in no humble manner, but shoulders back and head erect. She had bits of cotton flecked on her hair and I thought I saw an oily mark on her arm, and my impression was that she worked as a half-timer in the mill, and had been working that morning and being holidays now had the afternoon off.

Ben and Sam stared at her quite brazenly. I didn't because my Mother always impressed upon me that to stare was a most ignorant act. So I sort of squinted out of the corner of my eye – but to be honest I was just as curious as they were, only I tried not to show it.

The girl stretched herself, and in doing so she touched the handcart which half turned.

It could now be seen that she had been sitting on an upturned barrel, and in front of that was an empty orange-case set on its end, and there could be seen a jam-jar of water, and a box of paints and a sheet of white paper on which there was some bright colour. Then I saw the girl put something from her hand – it was a fine paint-brush – into the jar of water.

'Sufferin' mackerel,' said Ben, 'if she aren't paintin' and sketchin'!'

'Paintin' wut?' said Sam. At times Sam was inclined to be a bit on the slow side.

'A picture or summat,' said Ben. 'Wut else?'

'But wut picture is there 'ere?' asked Sam. 'I mean to sit down an' paint?'

Yes, that was the question, and it had puzzled me. And it baffled Ben for the moment.

'Don't ask me,' said Ben. 'All I know is that she's been paintin' or sketchin' or summat.'

'Aye,' said Sam, '– but *what*?'

'From here,' remarked Ben, who had sharp eyes, 'it looks like a sky and a rainbow.'

Sam looked upwards: 'You can hardly see the sky,' he said. 'As for a rainbow – I'll bet one's never been seen from this street.'

Ben himself seemed at a loss, and then he said: 'Happen she can see something we can't see.'

It struck me that may have been just about it.

**Bill Naughton**

Discussion point

This story puts across a strongly held belief or 'message'. What would you say that 'message' was?

Questions

1 In two or three sentences of your own describe the area the boys were visiting.
2 How can we tell that it was not the kind of area they lived in themselves?
3 What is Ben's attitude to the people who live there?
4 The girl 'was quite striking'. What does this mean, and why does he say it?
5 What is the difference in the way the three boys look at her?
6 Why were the boys surprised to see that she was painting?
7 Why were they even more surprised when they discovered *what* she was painting?
8 What is the meaning of the last sentence?

# Work and play

The swallow of summer, she toils all summer,
A blue-dark knot of glittering voltage,
A whiplash swimmer, a fish of the air.
    But the serpent of cars that crawls through the dust
    In shimmering exhaust
    Searching to slake
    Its fever in ocean
    Will play and be idle or else it will bust.

The swallow of summer, the barbed harpoon,
She flings from the furnace, a rainbow of purples,
Dips her glow in the pond and is perfect.
    But the serpent of cars that collapsed on the beach
    Disgorges its organs
    A scamper of colours
    Which roll like tomatoes
    Nude as tomatoes
    With sand in their creases
    To cringe in the sparkle of rollers and screech.

The swallow of summer, the seamstress of summer,
She scissors the blue into shapes and she sews it,
She draws a long thread and she knots it at corners.
    But the holiday people
    Are laid out like wounded
    Flat as in ovens
    Roasting and basting
    With faces of torment as space burns them blue.

Their heads are transistors
Their teeth grit on sand grains
Their lost kids are squalling
While man-eating flies
Jab electric shock needles but what can they do?

They can climb in their cars with raw bodies, raw faces
   And start up the serpent
   And headache it homeward
   A car full of squabbles
   And sobbing and stickiness
   With sand in their crannies
   Inhaling petroleum
   That pours from the foxgloves
   While the evening swallow
The swallow of summer, cartwheeling through crimson,
Touches the honey-slow river and turning
Returns to the hand stretched from under the eaves –
A boomerang of rejoicing shadow.

**Ted Hughes**

---

. . . . . . NEWSFLASH . . . . . .

---

In a dawn raid
early this morning
Gendarmes arrested
a family of four
found bathing
on a secluded beach
outside Swansea.

Later in the day
tracker dogs
led German police officers
to the scene of a picnic
near Brighton.
Salmonpaste sandwiches
and a thermos of tea
were discovered.
The picnickers however
escaped.

**Roger McGough**

# *My happiest holiday . . .*

was in 1904, when I was 12. My mother Constance was already well known as a Russian translator, and she was invited to visit Russia, and took me with her. We were invited to stay on a big estate and as soon as we had settled in, I was given a pony.

I'd never ridden before but I learned to stick on it quite soon, and then I was free to ride off any morning wherever I liked. It was the height of summer and the whole country was full of flowers – it was the rich black earth of central Russia.

I soon met some peasant boys, whose job it was to look after the hordes of horses. About the middle of the day one of the boys would make a big fire, and make a soup of roast millet: and all we other boys would carry a wooden spoon tied round our waists, and we would eat out of the common pot. I used to help by purloining a pat of butter or a bottle of oil from the house, and if we caught any fish in the lake that would go into the pot, too. I don't know what I would think about it now, but it was wonderful then.

These boys were absolutely friendly – they accepted me completely. They had this extraordinary quality of primitive Christianity – I've never seen it anywhere else. When we were having our soup, if an old beggar or pilgrim passed by, they would call out to him and share it with him, even if they'd never seen him before, and I believe during a famine, a whole village would die together, because they went on sharing out to the last. But there was nothing like famine there. The one thing people suffered from was the Government – it took part of their crops for taxes, it took them for soldiers for four years.

These boys taught me Russian: you learn a language best by talking with people. Then every day, when I felt it was time, I would say goodbye and ride back to the house up an avenue of lime trees and past a nest of little red-legged falcons, all of which was very exciting to me.

Much later I would have dinner with my mother and our host. On a very grand occasion there would be roast pig stuffed with buckwheat, but the thing I cared about was the sweet – an ice-cream the size of a big top hat, full of nuts and fruits. It was cylindrical, and you cut it in slices: quite delicious.

This was my best holiday, because I learned the most. I learned about Russia, and I learned how to ride. It was the best, because it was the strangest.

**David Garnett**

# Indian country

### Just back from the snake dance – tired out

The Hopi country is hideous – a clayey pale-grey desert with death-grey *mesas**  sticking up like broken pieces of ancient dry grey bread. And the hell of a lumpy trail for forty miles. Yet car after car lurched and bobbed and ducked across the dismalness, on Sunday afternoon.

Hotevilla is a scrap of a place with a plaza no bigger than a fair-sized back-yard: and the chief house on the square a ruin. But into this plaza finally three thousand onlookers piled. A mile from the village was improvised the official camping ground, like a corral with hundreds of black motor cars. Across the death-grey desert, bump and lurch, came strings of more black cars, like a funeral *cortège*. Till everybody had come – about three thousand bodies.

And all these bodies piled in the oblong plaza, on the roofs, in the ruined windows, and thick around on the sandy floor, under the old walls: a great crowd. There were Americans of all sorts, wild west and tame west, American women in pants, an extraordinary assortment of female breeches: and at least two women in skirts, relics of the last era. There were Navajo women in full skirts and velvet bodices: there were Hopi women in bright shawls: a Negress in a low-cut black blouse and a black sailor hat: various half-breeds: and all the men to match.

And what had they all come to see? come so far, over so weary a way to camp uncomfortably? To see a little bit of a snake dance in a plaza no bigger than a back-yard? Light grey-daubed antelope-priests (so-called) and a dozen black-daubed snake-priests (so-called). No drums, no pageantry. A hollow muttering. And then one of the snake-priests hopping slowly round with the neck of a pale, bird-like snake nipped between his teeth, while six elder priests dusted the six younger, snake-adorned priests with prayer feathers on the shoulders, hopping behind like a children's game. After a few little rounds the man set his snake on the sand, and away it steered, towards the massed spectators sitting around: and after it came a snake-priest with a snake stick, picked it up with a flourish from the shrinking crowd, and handed it to an antelope-priest in the background. The six young men renewed their snake as the eagle his youth – sometimes the youngest, a boy of fourteen or so, had a rattlesnake ornamentally dropping from his teeth, sometimes a racer, a thin whip snake, sometimes a heavier bull-snake, which

* mesas: flat-topped hills

wrapped its long end round his knee like a garter – till he calmly undid it. More snakes, till the priests at the back had little armfuls, like armfuls of silk stockings that were going to hang on the line to dry. When all the snakes had had their little ride in a man's mouth, and had made their little excursion towards the crowd, they were all gathered, like a real lot of wet silk stockings – say forty – or thirty – and left to wriggle all together for a minute in meal, corn-meal, that the women of the *pueblo* had laid down on the sand of the plaza. Then, hey presto! – they were snatched up like fallen washing, and the two priests ran away with them westward, down the *mesa*, to set them free among the rocks, at the snake-shrine.

And it was over. Navajos began to ride to the sunset, black motor-cars began to scuttle with their backs to the light. It was over.

And what had we come to see, all of us? Men with snakes in their mouths, like a circus? Nice clean snakes, all washed and cold-creamed by the priests (so-called). Like wet pale silk stockings. Snakes with little bird-like heads, that bit nobody, but looked more harmless than doves? And funny men with blackened faces and whitened jaws, like a corpse band?

A show? But it was a tiny little show, for all that distance.

Just a show! The south-west is the great playground for the white American. The desert isn't good for anything else. But it does make a fine national playground. And the Indian with his long hair and his bits of pottery and blankets and clumsy home-made trinkets, he's a wonderful live toy to play with. More fun than keeping rabbits, and just as harmless. Wonderful, really, hopping around with a snake in his mouth. Lots of fun! Oh, the wild west is lots of fun: the Land of Enchantment. Like being right inside the circus-ring: lots of sand, and painted savages jabbering, and snakes and all that. Come on, boys! Lots of fun! The great south-west, the national circus-ground. Come on boys; we've every bit as much right to it as anybody else. Lots of fun!

**D. H. Lawrence**

# *Navajo children, Canyon de Chelly, Arizona*

You sprouted from sand,
running, stopping, running;
beyond you tall red
tons of rock rested
on the feathery tamarisk.

Torn jeans, T-shirts
lope and skip, toes drum
and you're coming
full tilt
for the lollipops,

hopefully
arrive, daren't
look, for our stares
(your noses dribble)
prove too rude

in your silence,
can't break, either,
your upturned
monkey faces into smiles.
It's no joke

as you grope
up, up
to the driver's door, take
them reverently, the
lollipops –

your smallest, too small,
waited three
paces back, shuffling,
then provided,
evidently

by a sister on tiptoe who
takes his hand, helps
unwrap the sugar totem.
And we are swept
on, bouncing,

look back,
seeing walls
dwarf you. But how
could you get any
more thin, small, far?

**Christopher Middleton**

# Madeira Funchal from **£114**

**Madeira** – island paradise where the sun always shines and the people always smile. Rich in coastline, clifftops and mountains, Madeira offers the discerning holidaymaker that away-from-it-all vacation with a difference. Blue Horizon have chosen specially for *you* a range of hotels that between them cater for every taste. Whether you just want to laze beside the pool; explore the quaint narrow streets of Camara de Lobos or Camacha; hunt for souvenirs of basketwork or the world-famous embroidery: whatever your interest, Blue Horizon can offer you the best.

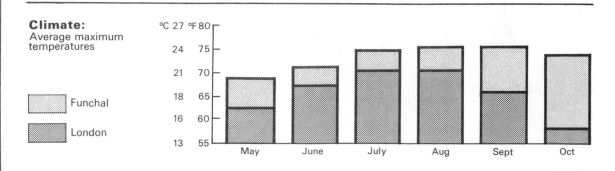

MADEIRA

Ribeira Brava
Camara de Lobos
**Funchal**
Santa Cruz

—— Roads

▒ Mountains

### Flying

Santa Cruz (*from Luton*)
3 hours 40 minutes

### Coach

Funchal (*from Santa Cruz*)
1 hour

0      10 miles

**Climate:**
Average maximum temperatures

▒ Funchal

▓ London

°C 27 °F 80 —
24   75
21   70
18   65
16   60
13   55

May   June   July   Aug   Sept   Oct

# BLUE HORIZON

## Booking

It's simple. All you have to do is choose your dates, choose your price/hotel, write us a letter enclosing the 10% deposit and leave the rest to us.

Blue Horizon reserve the right to apply a fuel and/or exchange rate surcharge between the dates of booking and departure. The deposit is non-returnable. The balance is due one calendar month before the date of the holiday. We also reserve the right to locate holidaymakers in a different hotel from that booked but of equivalent status, for any reasonable cause.

## Blue Horizon Hotels

# GREENE'S

Exotic gardens, 2 swimming pools, Sailing & fishing: own jetty & boats. Top class cuisine.

*All rooms have:*
balcony with sea view, bath, WC, twin beds.

*Supplements:*
single room £40
full board £48

# LA BAMBA

Rooftop pool & bar
2 bars
Garden lounge
Beautiful views
Central position

All rooms twin-bedded with bath, WC and balcony

*Supplements:*
single room £30
full board £30

# PARADISO

Bar
Swimming pool
Table tennis
Close to town

2/3-bedded rooms with bath/WC

*Supplements:*
single room £42
full board £21

## Prices

All prices are per person for one week. They include air/coach travel to and from Luton. Prices include shared use of room and half-board – breakfast and evening meal. See hotel details for single room and full board supplements.

| Month | Hotel ▶ Greene's | | La Bamba | | Paradiso | |
|---|---|---|---|---|---|---|
| | ADULT | CHILD | ADULT | CHILD | ADULT | CHILD |
| MAY | £256 | £200 | £206 | £156 | £175 | £125 |
| JUNE | 245 | 195 | 195 | 145 | 164 | 114 |
| JULY | 263 | 213 | 219 | 171 | 169 | 119 |
| AUGUST | 268 | 218 | 225 | 175 | 175 | 125 |
| SEPTEMBER | 263 | 213 | 219 | 171 | 169 | 119 |
| OCTOBER | 357 | 307 | 214 | 166 | 164 | 114 |

To calculate the charge for two weeks for each adult, add £120 to the rates shown for Greene's Hotel, £70 for La Bamba, and £40 for Paradiso. Add half these amounts for each child.

# Booking

You want to book a holiday for your family. Here are the details.

People travelling:   2 adults, 1 son, 1 daughter

Possible dates        15th–30th May
in these periods:     15th July–30th August
                      15th–30th October

Maximum money available: £1,000

**Decide:**   1   When you want to go. (Look at the temperature chart.)
2   Which hotel you would like to stay at.
3   How long you would like to stay.

**Work out:**   1   How much it would cost.
2   Whether you can afford it. (If not, change your plans!)
3   How much the deposit is.

**Write:**   a letter booking your holiday. The address to write to is:
The Manager
Blue Horizon
Delamere Street
London
W1X 6TG

# Complaints

1   You are the Manager of Blue Horizon. You receive this letter.

> 92 Deansway
> Cheltenham
> Glos.
> GL27 6MA
>
> The Manager
> Blue Horizon
> Delamere Street
> London W1X 6TG          23rd September 1982
>
> Dear Sir,
>       I wish to complain about a recent holiday we spent
> in Madeira, booked through your company.
>       We were booked into the La Bamba Hotel, which had
> been recommended to us by friends. When we reached Funchal, we
> were told that we had to stay at the Hotel Estrelita, which is
> 3 miles outside Funchal. The bus service was almost non-existent,
> the food was terrible; and the hotel was dirty.
>       This is not the hotel we had expected when we paid
> you a total of £590. I demand a refund of the money we paid.
>
>       Yours faithfully,
>       P. J. Clegg.

**Decide:** Is this a fair complaint? (Check with the brochure.)
Should you repay any money?
If so, how much?
If not, what are you going to do?

Then write the letter in reply. Make sure that your letter is correctly set out.

2 You recently had a Blue Horizon holiday in Funchal. A lot of things went wrong. Here are the facts:

Hotel: La Bamba
Dates: 8th–21st August
Family of 2 adults and 2 teenage boys.
Amount paid: £1,010
Problems: **a** Rooftop pool was out of use because it was being repaired.
**b** Only one bar was open because of staffing problems.
**c** In one of the rooms the bath didn't work.
**d** The balcony to the other room was dangerous, because half the railing was missing.

Write a letter of complaint.


# Be a travel agent

1 Choose a holiday resort. It may be a place you have visited; one that you have heard of: or it may be made up.
2 Decide what the main attractions of the resort are.
3 Make up some hotels and other holiday attractions.
4 Design a set of publicity material for your resort. You could include:

a brochure
a local tourist guide
a map
a poster
advertisements for hotels, sports and leisure facilities, and other attractions.

**hol-i-day** ('hɒlɪ,dei,-dɪ) *n.* **1.** (*often pl.*) *chiefly Brit.* **a.** a period in which a break is taken from work or studies for rest, travel, or recreation. U.S. word: **vacation. b.** (*as modifier*): *a holiday mood.* **2.** a day on which work is suspended by law or custom, such as a religious festival, bank holiday, etc. Related adj.: **ferial. 3.** any of several festivals commemorating major events in Israelite or Jewish history or days connected with such festivals. ~*vb.* **4.** (*intr.*) *Chiefly Brit.* to spend a holiday. [Old English *hāligdæg*, literally: holy day]

**hol-i-day camp** *n. Brit.* a place, esp. one at the seaside, providing accommodation, recreational facilities, etc., for holiday-makers.

**hol-i-day-maker** *n. Brit.* a person who goes on holiday. U.S. equivalents: **vacationer, vacationist.**

*Collins English Dictionary*

**Questions**

Answer these questions as fully as you can. They ask for your own opinions and you should give reasons for your opinions whenever possible.

1 Why do people have holidays?
2 What does the word *holiday* mean to you?
3 What would be your ideal holiday?
4 The idea of the annual holiday of two or three weeks is not very old. How much difference has it made to people's lives?
5 Do you think people should be able to have longer holidays than they do at present?
6 Would you like to have 52 weeks holiday a year?

**Word study**

Following the pattern of the dictionary extract above, write a detailed definition of one of these words:

labour   work   leisure   relax

Remember to give all possible meanings of the word you choose.

**Research**

Do your own opinion poll about holidays. Try to find out from people their ideas about an ideal holiday. Make up a list of questions to ask them. As you interview each person, record the answers you are given. Write a report on what you discover.

# THE CHILDREN'S CRUSADE

scenes from the play by Paul Thompson

The Crusades took place during the Middle Ages. They were a series of military expeditions by Christian armies from Europe, who wanted to win back the Holy Land from the Moslems. At this time Christians believed that the parts of Palestine where Jesus had lived and died should be controlled by them, so they set out to conquer them. They were successful: the First Crusade ended, after much bloodshed, with the capture of Jerusalem in 1099 A.D. The Moslems fought back, however, and by 1190 the Christians had been almost completely driven out of Palestine. From then on the Crusades had less and less to do with the Holy Land and more and more to do with a struggle for power and money. The Fourth Crusade set off in 1202, but instead of going to Palestine, it diverted to the Christian cities of Zara and Constantinople, which were captured and looted. In this way, a movement which had begun with high ideals sank into a series of squalid and money-grubbing quarrels. When news of the Fourth Crusade reached France and Germany there were many people, especially young people, who were very angry about this. So started the Children's Crusade.

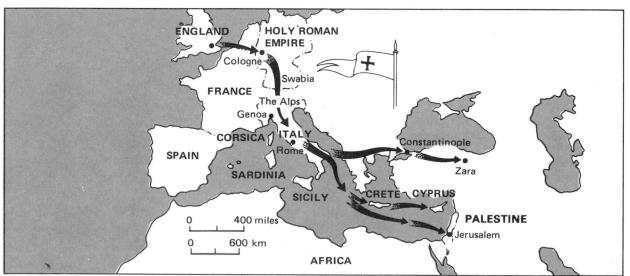

# *Scene 1*

The scenes that follow come from a play that was written for the National Youth Theatre. They form about one third of the whole play and tell the beginning of the story. There is a summary of the remainder of the play at the end of the unit.

In a period of crisis and confusion POPE INNOCENT III proclaims the Fourth Crusade.

POPE INNOCENT III *and* SIX CARDINALS. *The speeches are punctuated by loud bells and at certain points a crash of a gong.*

POPE INNOCENT III: You Christians who call yourselves Christian, you who are engaged in wars and quarrels one with another, you do most sinfully neglect the true and sacred field for your valour. Though we have all the cares of all the churches upon us, still our chief anxiety is for the liberation of the Lord's sepulchre in the Holy City of Jerusalem. The Sanctity, the wonder of the Land of Promise, the Land chosen of God, of this Land the foul Infidel is now lord!

FIRST CARDINAL: The Holy Temple is become a den of thieves!

SECOND CARDINAL: The Holy City, the dwelling place of devils!

THIRD CARDINAL: The Churches, even the Holy Sepulchre itself are become stalls for cattle!

FOURTH CARDINAL: In the Land of Our Saviour, Christian men are massacred.

FIFTH CARDINAL: Christian women are ravished.

FIRST CARDINAL
SIXTH CARDINAL } Children slaughtered within the Holy precincts!

SECOND CARDINAL: You Christian men, you make war upon each other, when you are called to be soldiers of Christ!

ALL CARDINALS: To fight for the Lord in the Land of His Birth!

THIRD CARDINAL: The Saviour Himself shall be your leader.

FOURTH CARDINAL: He shall be your guide in battle.

FIFTH CARDINAL: You shall march from victory to victory.

ALL CARDINALS: In the Glory of His Love!

    *Enter the* OLD CRUSADER. *He should stand in a separate area from the Cardinals. His style of speech should be low-key and naturalistic.*

OLD CRUSADER: From the very beginning we were in the hands of the Venetian merchants. We were unable to meet the full cost of our passage and so we had little choice but to comply with their wishes. They would not take us to the Holy Land, but took us instead to their rival merchant city of Zara. And there the Crusaders rushed through the whole city, seizing gold, silver, horses and mules, and looting the houses that were full of costly things. That was Zara. It was a Christian City.

SIXTH CARDINAL: The wealth of your enemies shall be yours.

FOURTH CARDINAL: You shall plunder their treasurers.

SECOND CARDINAL: You serve a Commander who will not permit his troops to go hungry.

FIFTH CARDINAL: Nor will he deny you a just reward for your services.

FIRST CARDINAL: There is no crime . . .

THIRD CARDINAL: Murder.

SECOND CARDINAL: Adultery.

FOURTH CARDINAL: Robbery.

SIXTH CARDINAL: Arson.

ALL CARDINALS: Which shall not be redeemed by this act of obedience to God!

OLD CRUSADER: We never reached the Holy Land. The merchants would take us no farther than to Constantinople, the capital of Christian Civilization in the East. The treasures of that city proved too great a temptation. Amid the ruins of Constantinople, we consoled ourselves with the spoils of war. But the victory really belonged to Venice. The merchants had achieved what they had always sought . . . commercial supremacy over all their rivals.

POPE INNOCENT III: Absolution for all sins. Absolution without penance to all who take up arms in this Sacred cause. We promise eternal life to all those who suffer the Glorious calamity of death in the Holy Land. For the Crusader shall pass at once into Paradise.

FIRST CARDINAL: Let every city.

SECOND CARDINAL: Every Count.

FOURTH CARDINAL: Every Baron.

THIRD CARDINAL: Send forth an army of soldiers to rid the Holy Land for ever of the Usurping Infidel.

ALL CARDINALS: You are the soldiers of Christ! Our prayers are for your success.

POPE INNOCENT III: It is the will of God!

ALL CARDINALS: It is the will of God! It is the will of God! It is the will of God!

*Exit the* OLD CRUSADER.

**Questions to think and talk about**

*The Church's attitude*

1 What does the Church want people to do?
2 Why?
3 How does the Church believe the Crusaders will benefit personally?

*The Old Crusader's attitude*

4 What Crusade has he been on?
5 What happened?
6 Why?
7 What is his opinion of what the Church says?

**Writing**

The Old Crusader meets one of the Cardinals. They argue about the Crusade. Write their argument.

# Scene 2

Cologne 1212 – German children respond to the corruption and failure of the Fourth Crusade

*Two boys, aged about fifteen, are addressing a crowd of* CHILDREN. *The* CHILDREN *are kneeling. Throughout the scene they should hum, creating a ritualistic effect. This 'drone' should swell at significant points in the scene.*

NICHOLAS (*arms outstretched, eyes closed*): I waited patiently for the Lord and He came to me. I put my trust in Him and He received me. And into my mouth He put a new song. (*He opens his eyes.*) Children of Germany, hear me – the Lord is come amongst us.

> *More* CHILDREN *enter.*

Praise God, you children of Cologne, for you shall see the Holy Land. You shall reach Jerusalem! You shall win the Cross!

> *More* CHILDREN *enter.*

FRANCIS: We have seen our fathers fail. We have seen them betray their Crusade. Merchants got rich! Noblemen grabbed land! But the Holy Cross remains in the hands of the heathen. The rich are unworthy of the Holy Land. Children of Germany, only you can triumph where your fathers have failed. Your hands are not stained with blood! The Lord calls you to join the Crusade!

NICHOLAS (*arms outstretched, eyes closed*): O Lord, forgive our fathers, they have made this world a sinful place. (*He opens his eyes.*) Jesus spoke to me saying – 'Go ye in peace unto Jerusalem and ye shall win the Cross. For as you are young so are you innocent. As you are poor so are you blessed. You shall need no weapons for I am with you, and my light shall be by your side.' Jesus will be our guide and our path shall be filled with flowers. Butterflies will float above us, and the beasts of the field will follow us. And when we reach the sea . . . then shall God perform a miracle. The sea will part before us and we shall walk across to the Holy Land! Our eyes shall see Jerusalem. Our faith shall convert the heathen. And our love shall win back the One True Cross!

FRANCIS: All who would follow Nicholas – step forward and take the vow! Join the Holy Crusade of Children!

> ONE BOY *steps forward and kneels before* NICHOLAS.

NICHOLAS (*swears in the first boy*): Do you promise to Christ Our Lord and to All the Saints, that you will fulfil the Sacred Task entrusted to you, that you will go to Jerusalem, that you will win the Cross?

BOY I: I do.

NICHOLAS: Lord Jesus bless thy servant. Bless him and keep him safe always. – Amen. (ANOTHER BOY *steps forward. He kneels before* NICHOLAS.) (*Swears in the second boy* ) Do you promise to Christ Our Lord and to All the Saints, that you will fulfil the Sacred Task entrusted to you, that you will go to Jerusalem, that you will win the Cross?

BOY 2: I do.

NICHOLAS: Lord Jesus bless thy servant, bless him and keep him safe always. – Amen.

*The vows ceremony continues as a silent mime. The ritualistic 'humming' continues.*

'LEAVE-TAKINGS' – *These scenes should develop from improvizations. Most of these scenes take place 'around' the town square, they could be lit by individual spotlights.*

BOY *meets* GIRL.

JOHN: Is that Nicholas?

LESLEY: He's wonderful, isn't he?

JOHN: Are you going with him?

LESLEY: Yes.

JOHN: On your own? (*pause*). My name's John.

MOTHER *and two* SONS.

JANE: Goodbye, Martin.

COLIN: Goodbye, Mum.

JANE: Goodbye, Colin. Shall I say anything to your father?

MARTIN: No. Don't bother!

*Two* BROTHERS *and a* STRANGER

PATRICK: Look, here's another one . . . mugs!

TERRY: Is this the great gathering?

PATRICK: Here, are you going to walk through the water?

TERRY: We're going to Jerusalem, are you coming?

STEVE: Yeah.

PATRICK (*to* TERRY): Push off.

*Two* SKYVERS

ANDREW: Are you going then?

TREVOR: No, too much walking.

ANDREW: It's better than working.

TREVOR: Yeah, that's a point.

*Return to two* BROTHERS – *'Walk through water'*

STEVE: Come on. Let's go!

PATRICK: No.

STEVE: Everyone else is going.

PATRICK: All right. Let's you and me walk through the water.

*The* COUNTRY BOY *and the* CITY BOY

MICHAEL: You're from the country, aren't you?

TONY: How did you know?

MICHAEL: You won't get far with no shoes. Why are you going?

TONY: No work. You?

MICHAEL: No jobs round here.

*A* MOTHER *says goodbye to her* DAUGHTER *and* SON

LINDY: It's a pilgrimage, it's not a war.

DEBBIE: I'm frightened.

LINDY: You've got your brother.

JONATHAN (*looking at* NICHOLAS): We're with God.

*The old* CRUSADER *and two* BOYS

OLD CRUSADER: Look, lads, I'll tell you this for nothing. Don't go.

PAUL: It'll be different this time.

ROBERT: We're going in peace.

OLD CRUSADER: Yeah, I've heard that before – set out in peace, come home in pieces.

PAUL: Is that a joke?

OLD CRUSADER: I wish it was.

NICHOLAS: Lord Jesus have mercy on us thy children. Give us thy blessing as we set out in thy service. Help us to be worthy of Thee.

*The humming stops.*

ALL: We promise to Christ Our Lord and to All the Saints, that we shall do His Holy will. That we shall live as He did live and go where He did go. We promise, unto *death*, that we shall fulfil the Sacred Task entrusted to us, that we shall go to Jerusalem, that we shall win the Cross.

NICHOLAS: Amen. (NICHOLAS's FATHER *approaches his son.*) Goodbye, father.

FATHER: Nicholas . . . the Lord be with you. (*They embrace.*) May God protect you.

NICHOLAS: He will father. He will.

NICHOLAS *walks through the* CROWD. *They are still kneeling, they reach out to touch him. Music introduction.*

SONG: 'THE SONG OF THE CONFIDENCE OF YOUTH.'
Stand aside, all you merchants and bankers.
Stand aside, all you compromised preachers.
Stand aside, all you soldiers of war.
We can see what you really stand for.

We have lived in your world of corruption.
We've seen more than you taught us to see.
Now we're no longer fooled by excuses.
We won't be what you want us to be.

We are young and eternally hopeful,
And hope is a powerful thing.
We are young and although we're not perfect,
At least we try and we never give in!

FOUR BOYS *bring in a chair.* NICHOLAS *sits in it. The* CHILDREN *cheer as he is raised shoulder high. They leave singing.*

Stand aside, all you merchants and bankers
Stand aside, all you soldiers of war
Stand aside, you compromised preachers
We can see what you really stand for.

*The* PARENTS *shake hands with Nicholas's father, they wave to their* CHILDREN *and cheer as they leave. The* OLD CRUSADER *watches it all, he exits slowly in dismay.*

| Questions to think and talk about | | |
|---|---|---|
| | 1 | What do Francis and Nicholas want the children to do? |
| | 2 | In what ways is this different from any other Crusade? |
| | 3 | What impression do you get of Nicholas? |
| | 4 | What impressions do you get of the children who join the Crusade? |

| Leave-takings | | |
|---|---|---|
| | 1 | Improvize or write two short scenes to fit into the 'Leave-takings' section. Try to make them as different from each other as you can. |
| | 2 | With a partner rehearse your scenes for performance. |

# Scene 3

In the Duchy of Suabia – Principles are put into practice

*A farm near the Alps. Two sons are harnessed to their father's plough. The*
*FARMER guides the plough as they complete one furrow, turn, and begin*
*another. In the distance, we hear the sound of CHILDREN singing as the*
*Crusade marches past. The boys stop.*

FARMER: Keep moving.

KLAUS (*the older son*): Come on.

> *They continue working.*

FARMER: What we could do with now is a nice drop of rain. That'd
dampen their spirits for 'em (*pause*). I've had enough of all this.
Up and down to the Holy Land. Who do they think they are?
Trampling over my beans. The years I've put up with it. Can't
they find another way through the Alps?

> *When they complete this furrow, they stop. They have now reached*
> *the spot where they left their jackets, food and water. They take a drink.*
Half of 'em ain't Crusaders at all you know. Vagrants. Beggars.
Always after something. They'd have the shirt off yer back if you
let 'em.

DAVID (*the younger son*): It's a sin not to help 'em.

FARMER: Don't I know it.

DAVID: But they're children.

FARMER: Then they ought to know better.

KLAUS: Let's go back to work.

DAVID: I shouldn't be working here. My place is over there, with
them!

FARMER: Your place is 'ere. Get moving.

> *They work. The song dies away.*

DAVID (*stops*): They've gone. They never came near us.

FARMER: Keep going straight! How many times do I have to tell yer?
Look at it. A right bloody mess we're making here (*pause*). Come
on now. A nice straight line.

> *They work in silence.*

DAVID: My back hurts.

FARMER: Soon be finished.

> *They work in silence. SIMON enters. He is a Crusader, he stands on*
> *the newly ploughed section.*

SIMON: Hello, friend.

FARMER: I just done there!

SIMON: Sorry.

FARMER: What do you want?

SIMON: Would you like to help the Crusade, sir?

FARMER: Eh? . . . Look here, if it wasn't for me there wouldn't be no Crusades. I keep 'em going.

SIMON: You're a good man. We've been on the road for a month, we're tired and hungry.

FARMER: What do you want?

SIMON: Water. If you have any.

> DAVID *fetches the water and carries it towards them. The* FARMER *takes it from his son and gives it to* SIMON.

Thank you, sir. The Lord rewards those who help Crusaders.

FARMER: And punishes them who don't. (*To sons.*) Back to work.

> *They start to work.*

SIMON: Excuse me, sir . . .

FARMER (*stops*): I thought so. Something else.

SIMON: Do you have any bread?

FARMER: Yes, thanks. (*Pause. To* KLAUS.) Give him a slice.

> DAVID *hurries to bread and takes half a loaf to* SIMON.

DAVID: Take me with you.

FARMER: What was that?

DAVID: I want to go with you.

FARMER: Get back. (*To* SIMON.) On your way!

DAVID: You can't make me!

SIMON: Your son wants to come with us.

FARMER: He's staying here.

SIMON: When we marched down the Rhine Valley, crowds waved at us and cheered. They brought us food, they gave us shelter . . .

FARMER: He's my son.

SIMON: . . . at every town, children flocked to us, *their* parents gave them up willingly.

FARMER: I need my son.

SIMON: More than we need him?

DAVID (*to* FARMER): You don't need me. You've got Klaus. I'll run away. You can't stop me.

FARMER: You won't.

SIMON: Why won't you let him go?

FARMER: I need him! We're poor, we've given everything we can. We can't afford any more. I sold a horse, my ox . . . what else? My land? Should I give that up too? I need labour!

DAVID: There's nothing for me here. Your land goes to Klaus!

FARMER: Look, David, why should you fight in a foreign land? You can serve God just as well here at home. If it was just a question of . . . of crossing a stream, yes, I'd let you go willingly, happily. You could jump across! Wade through it if you like! But the Alps! You won't survive! . . . And if you reach the sea . . . (*He turns to* SIMON.) God is everywhere, to you He may only be in Jerusalem, but to me He's here in Germany too!

DAVID (*to* SIMON): Let's go.

FARMER: Wait! Put down the bread. Put it down! And the water. (SIMON *does so.*) Right. In my barn I've got a sack of grain, I was keeping it. I got blankets (*To* KLAUS.) Go and get 'em. (KLAUS *hurries off. The* FARMER *collects the water and bag of food, and he lays them at* SIMON's *feet.*) Take these. Now you can have all that and what's in my barn. Take my jacket, you must be cold in the mountains. (*He takes it off.*) You can have all these. But leave me my son.

SIMON: Is that everything you have?

FARMER: That's everything I have.

SIMON: I respect your sacrifice. It speaks well of the love you have for your son . . .

FARMER: You say you're hungry . . . there's meat in there. A sack of grain. If you take him you get nothing. Understand? No food, nothing. Less than nothing – you take on another mouth to feed. (*Pause*). Now choose. My son or my goods?

SIMON: You have little understanding of our cause. First of all we are not going off to war, we go in peace to put an end to war. Secondly, we intend to make no compromises. We shall not repeat the mistakes our fathers made.

FARMER: Choose!

SIMON: The choice is very easy. Your son.

*And this should be a difficult choice for Simon.*

FARMER: Take him.

DAVID: I'm sorry, father.

FARMER: Go!

*They go.*

(*Shouting after them.*) Yes. All you 'pilgrims', you think you're so holy. You think you're so bloody holy! . . . How is it then, that when you come back you're just bandits? . . . Eh? . . . You tell me!

*Pause. Enter* KLAUS *with sack and blankets.*

KLAUS: They've gone. You let him go? (*He puts down the sack and looks at the food and water.*) Now he'll starve, like the rest of 'em.
*Silence.*

FARMER: Indoors. It's starting to rain.
*They go.*

**Writing**

David goes off with Simon. As they travel, they talk. David wants to know all about the Crusade: who is on it, where they have all come from; where they are going next; what they will do. Simon answers his questions and explains the aims of the Crusade.

Write their conversation.

**Group work**

This short scene must have been repeated in many homes all over France and Germany. Parents tried to persuade their children not to go on the Crusade, but without success. Make up a similar scene to be read or acted by the members of your group. It can be written down, or built up through improvization.

# Scene 4

The Alps – difficulties are overcome

*Enter the* CRUSADERS.

SONG: 'THE SONG OF OVERCOMING DIFFICULTIES'
There's not a thing that we don't know about these mountains,
We know that children cry when they're alone,
We have learned to live in terrible conditions,
But we learned that lesson, long ago, at home.

Now it's cold. Oh, how the night is freezing.
But there's nothing we can do to alter that.
There's no food. So now we shall go hungry.
But then again, that's just another fact.

There's not a thing that we don't know about these mountains,
We've seen the stains of blood beneath our feet,
But we know that in the end when we have nothing,
Our hope alone will keep us from defeat.

Now it's cold. Oh, how the night is freezing.
But there's nothing we can do to alter that.
There's no food. So now we shall go hungry.
But then again, that's just another fact.

> *During the last verse,* NICHOLAS *enters, he is carried in his chair by* FOUR ATTENDANTS. *When the song ends the* CHILDREN *sit down in groups around the stage. It is night, they huddle together for warmth.* FRANCIS *goes to* NICHOLAS *who remains in his chair.*

FRANCIS: Here you are, Nicholas. (*He offers* NICHOLAS *some bread.*)

NICHOLAS: Is that the last of the bread? (*Pause.*) You have it, Francis.

FRANCIS: No. It's more important that you eat. (*Pause.*) Please.

> NICHOLAS *refuses the bread.* FRANCIS *takes a lantern and leaves to review the 'troops'.*
>
> 'HARDSHIP SCENES' – *These scenes should be developed from improvizations.*
>
> *A* BOY *and a* GIRL *are nursing an exhausted girl*

LINDY: Just keep her warm.

> FRANCIS *approaches.*

FRANCIS: Is she all right?

LINDY: No she isn't.

FRANCIS: Get her a blanket.

BILL: Where from?

FRANCIS: Ask.

*JOHN and LESLEY, the two lovers, offer one of their blankets.*

JOHN: Here you are.

BILL: What are you going to do?

LESLEY: We only need one.

*BILL and LINDY cover up the sick girl. FRANCIS moves on.*

*FRANCIS approaches four BOYS huddled together. (ANDREW, TREVOR, PAUL and ROBERT)*

FRANCIS: Have you had anything to eat?

TREVOR: No.

FRANCIS: Here.

*He gives them the remaining crust of bread.*

ANDREW: Better than nothing.

*They eat furiously, FRANCIS moves on.*

*FRANCIS approaches a GIRL and a BOY, neither has a blanket*

STEPHANIE (*to* PETER): It's warmer walking, isn't it.

PETER: Yes.

FRANCIS: Haven't you got a blanket between you?

PETER: No. Perhaps we could . . . snuggle up together.

FRANCIS: Yes. (*To* STEPHANIE.) Is that all right?

STEPHANIE: Yes.

*They cuddle up to each other. FRANCIS moves on.*

*Two BROTHERS under one blanket*

*FRANCIS approaches someone covered by a blanket. He lifts up a corner of the blanket.*

FRANCIS: Good night.

*A head pops out.*

RICHARD: 'Night.

*FRANCIS goes. Another head pops out.*

PIP: Good night!

*FRANCIS smiles, he moves on.*

*BROTHER and SISTER. Next to them is DENNIS, he is injured, they have carried him.*

FRANCIS (*to* DENNIS): Are you all right?

DENNIS (*crying*): Yeah, I'm all right.

IAN: I'm carrying him.

CAROLINE (*to* FRANCIS): How much farther is it?

FRANCIS: A long way yet.

CAROLINE: How far?

FRANCIS: I don't know.

CAROLINE: Nicholas knows though, doesn't he?

FRANCIS: We'll reach the sea. We'll reach Jerusalem.

> FRANCIS *moves on.*

TWO BROTHERS
> STEVE *is crying with the cold,* PATRICK *is trying to warm him.*

PATRICK: Quiet!

> STEVE *is crying.* PATRICK *rubs his hands.*

FRANCIS: How is he?

> *Pause. They ignore Francis.*

Can I help?

> *Pause.*

Get some sleep.

> *The* LIGHT FADES. FRANCIS *crosses to* NICHOLAS *who remains in his chair. Their scene takes place in a spotlight.*

FRANCIS: Where are we, Nicholas?

NICHOLAS: Here (*pause*). We are here.

FRANCIS: No . . . How far is it?

NICHOLAS: I don't know.

FRANCIS: Look, they're frightened. They're cold, they're hungry. We've brought them a long way, Nicholas, they trust us! . . . How can we ask them to go on?

NICHOLAS: We must go on.

FRANCIS: How?

NICHOLAS: Faith, Francis, Faith. The faith that brought us this far. Hope. Love. We don't need anything else.

FRANCIS: Yes, but tomorrow . . . if we find no food . . . what then? They'll die.

NICHOLAS: We are in the hands of the Lord Jesus. We are perfectly safe. Perfectly safe.

FRANCIS: But they'll die! . . . I'm frightened, Nicholas . . . if we should fail . . . we must *do* something.

NICHOLAS: Sit down, Francis. Sit down.

FRANCIS: What can we *do*?

NICHOLAS: Nothing (*pause*). Please sit down (*pause*). If you think we need help . . . I'll pray for help.

> FRANCIS *sits at Nicholas's feet, he puts his head in his lap.*

NICHOLAS *strokes Francis's hair.* FADE LIGHTS SLOWLY.

Questions to think
and talk about

The Crusaders are suffering:
1 How do they react to their difficulties?
2 What does Francis feel and do about it?
3 How does Nicholas react?
4 What does this scene tell us about the characters of the two leaders?

Hardship scenes

1 Improvize or write two short scenes to fit into this section.
2 With a partner, or members of your group, rehearse your scenes for performance.

# Scene 5

Northern Italy – the ends and the means

*Enter the* MARQUIS OF MONTSERRAT. FRANCIS *is at his side,* DAVID *is with him. Behind them is a group of the children.* NICHOLAS *is not there.*

MARQUIS: I'm quite prepared to leave the arrangements to you. Organize yourselves as you think best.

FRANCIS: Thank you.

MARQUIS: What's this?

*He picks up some barley to test their knowledge.*

DAVID (*comes forward*): Barley. (*He examines it.*) Two-rowed barley. It's got short roots so you don't need deep-ploughing, a light soil. You test the ripeness with your finger-nail, like that. You'll be using this for malting I expect.

MARQUIS: Probably, I don't take a personal interest in my estate, not to that extent. (*Pause.*) Well, I'm sure you know what you're doing. You've seen the orchard, the vineyard. I'll leave you to get on with it.

DAVID: What about the people who normally do this work. Where are they?

MARQUIS: Ah . . . well, they're with the Duke of Savoy now. Yes, over there. I'm afraid they left me for him . . . left me in the lurch, so to speak.

DAVID: I see.

FRANCIS: When do we get paid?

MARQUIS: When you've finished. You get a meal every night, and . . . er . . . that's all. Any questions?

FRANCIS: No.

MARQUIS: Jolly good, I'll leave you to it.

*He goes.*

FRANCIS: Well done, David!

DAVID: The man's a fool. He doesn't deserve this land. It's not used properly.

FRANCIS: Never mind. We're getting paid and that's all that counts right now.

*Enter* NICHOLAS *and* ENTOURAGE. *He is carried in his chair.*

FRANCIS: It won't take us long, Nicholas.

NICHOLAS: We shouldn't work! All this is keeping us from our duty.

FRANCIS: If we don't eat, we won't have the strength to get there. We must work. (*Pause. To the* CHILDREN.) Come on.

NICHOLAS *watches as they work.*

## MIME SEQUENCE

*Barley Field*

1 Some children cut the barley with sickles.
2 Others gather it and bind it into sheaves.
3 Others build stacks with the sheaves.

They work in a steady rhythm. Introducing sounds, swishes and clicks. They hum a tune.

*Orchard*

The children take up the rhythm and tune.

1 Some children are picking apples.
2 Others are filling baskets and sorting.
3 Others are loading a wagon.

The tune builds up.

*Vineyard*

The children take up the rhythm and tune.

1 Some children are picking grapes and filling baskets.
2 Others carry the baskets to the yard.
3 Others are treading the grapes.

The tune builds up.

All around the theatre there is now purposeful activity, a strong steady rhythm of work, everybody humming and 'ahing' a tune. Positive enjoyment in their labour.

*Sudden entrance of* SIX PEASANTS, *with cudgels, scythes, pitchforks.*

PEASANT LEADER: You kids, clear off! This is our work!

*The work stops. Silence.*

You heard me. Clear off!

FRANCIS: Who are you?

PEASANT LEADER: Never mind who I am. You're taking our work away!

PEASANT 1: Shove off!

DAVID: I'm sorry, but we understood no one worked here. The man said he couldn't get anyone.

PEASANT LEADER: Don't make me laugh.

DAVID: He said they'd gone to the Duke of Savoy.

PEASANT 1: Lies! We always work here. All our families work here. We do the harvest and the threshing, that's six months' work!

FRANCIS: We're not threshing. Just the harvest. We'll be gone in a week.

PEASANT 2: Oh yeah? You're taking the food out of our mouths!

PEASANT 1: We need this work!

FRANCIS: So do we!

> *Pause.*

PEASANT: Look, mate, nothing against you personally, but you know what he's doing, don't you? You don't know the Marquis of Montserrat like we know him. He's got you on the cheap. He's using you to get at us.

FRANCIS: Then your argument's with him.

PEASANT LEADER: Don't get clever, sonny, we need this work, we rely on it.

FRANCIS: So do we! We're going to Jerusalem, to free the Holy Land. To baptize the Infidel. You're interfering with the will of God!

PEASANT LEADER: What?

PEASANT 1: What's he talking about?

> *The* PEASANTS *discuss the situation.*

DAVID: We can't take their work, Francis!

CRUSADER 1: No. They've got to get through the winter.

FRANCIS: What about us? We've got to get to the Holy Land.

CRUSADER 2: We need it more than they do.

CRUSADER 3: We've got to eat too!

CRUSADER 4: There's more of us, come on.

DAVID: We can't do it! It's their work! can't you see what's happening? . . . Nicholas tell them! (*Pause.*) Come on, you must . . . you can't just sit there!

> *Silence.* NICHOLAS *adopts his 'Guru' pose.*

FRANCIS: We are working here. We need food! To get food we need money, to get money – we've *got* to work! Our task is to get to Jerusalem! Everything else comes second! – there's no choice . . . work!

> *Silence.* FRANCIS *approaches the* PEASANTS.

PEASANT LEADER: Are you going?

FRANCIS: No.

PEASANT LEADER: Well, you asked for this then, sonny.

> *Just as the scuffle begins . . . enter the* MARQUIS.

MARQUIS: Mascolo! Get off my land!

> *They stop.*

Go on. Get going. And you, Simonetti. Off!

PEASANT LEADER: What are these kids doing here?

MARQUIS: They work here. I employ them!

PEASANT LEADER: But we do this.

PEASANT 1 (*to* PEASANT LEADER): Come on.

> *They start to go.*

MARQUIS: If you don't clear off right now, you'll never work here again. This is my land, I do what I like with it. Clear off! Do you want to lose the threshing as well?

PEASANT LEADER: All right . . . But you wait, we'll never work for you again!

> *They all go.*

MARQUIS (*laughs*): You will, Mascolo, you will. (*He laughs.*) You need me and you know it!

> *Silence.*

(*To* CHILDREN.) Well, get on with it then.

> *He goes.* DAVID *looks at the two 'leaders'. The* CHILDREN *go back to work and finally* DAVID *joins in too.* NICHOLAS *remains aloof.*

## MIME SEQUENCE

*Barley Field – orchard – vineyard*

> *In total silence they repeat the same actions, but this time with no co-ordination. No pleasure.*

**Questions to think and talk about**

1 What is Nicholas' opinion of the Crusaders working? Why?
2 Who should be allowed to do the work: the Crusaders or the peasants? Why?
3 How do the Crusaders feel at the end of the scene? Why?

**Writing**

On the next page there is a summary of the rest of the story of the play. Before you read it, think about what has happened so far: what do you think is likely to happen to the children from now on? Write down your ideas of how the story may develop and how it may end. Try to give the reasons for what you decide.

# *The rest of the story*

The children reach the Italian city of Genoa. Here they see the sea for the first time. Nicholas has told them that the water will open up and that they will then be able to walk to Palestine on the sea bed. (God has revealed this to him in a dream.) The sea does not divide, however, and the children are left to camp outside Genoa, surviving as best they can. Two merchants, Porcus and Ferreus, offer them five ships to take them to the Holy Land. Francis jumps at the idea, but Nicholas refuses, because he still believes in his miracle. They quarrel and separate.

Nicholas takes half the Crusaders on through Italy. He shares the leadership with David, the farmer's son. Then they, too, quarrel and separate because David wants to lead an army and get his own way by force. He and his group become bandits. Meanwhile the group who stayed with Francis have been tricked by Porcus and Ferreus and have been sold into slavery. They become the personal property of Sultan Al Kamil in Egypt. Nicholas leads his group to Rome, where he has an audience with Pope Innocent III. The Pope persuades him to lead the Crusaders back to their homes. When they get back to Cologne, a huge crowd is waiting. They are very angry with Nicholas and almost attack him. They are persuaded not to and turn instead on his father whom, in their anger, they lynch. The play ends with the surviving Crusaders singing a song of lament about their failure.

## Follow-up activities

**Discussion**  The ideas and ideals of the Crusades may seem very strange and remote today. In the thirteenth century, many young people believed strongly in the purpose and ideals of the Crusades. What ideals or beliefs today inspire young people in a similar way? Can you imagine a modern 'Children's Crusade'? Where would it go? What could it do? What problems might arise?

**Writing**
1  Write the diary of one of the children on the thirteenth-century crusade.
2  You are one of the survivors. Eventually you reach home and meet your parents. Tell the story of that meeting. Either as a story with conversation or in the form of a script.
3  Write the story of a modern crusade.

**Group work**  Choose one of the events described in the summary at the top of this page. Make up a scene about it for the play. You can write it down or develop it through improvization. Rehearse your scene for performance.

# Section B: Using language

This section looks at some of the ways in which we use language. The final twelve pages form a quick reference section on basic points in punctuation, grammar and presentation.

**Contents**

# Talking and writing

## No cheer, Kevin

A  Liverpool showed only touches of their old form and fluency but that was enough to wreck Kevin Keegan's Anfield homecoming. Keegan, and disappointing Southampton, were never in it as a superb early goal by Ray Kennedy gave Liverpool the spark of confidence they have lacked in recent weeks.

Liverpool's defence played with new assurance and the restored partnership of Hansen and Thompson had a relatively easy afternoon. Wells reacted sharply in the fortieth minute to save from McDermott, and Irwin should have buried a header after a marvellous centre from Dalglish a few minutes later.

A second goal had to come, however, and McDermott provided it. A shot by Alan Kennedy was deflected to Irwin. His shot was stopped by Wells, but McDermott was on hand to finish it off. Liverpool nearly got a third soon after, but Nicholl was on the line to head away a shot by McDermott after Dalglish and Alan Kennedy had carved another opening.

B  McDermott just outside the Southampton penalty area. McDermott holds. Plays a lovely long pass to Lee and Lee is given offside. This time the crowd is absolutely furious. The linesman with the red flag, who for his benefit shall remain anonymous, has again given an offside decision when it seemed at . . . er . . . the very least questionable. The crowd won't like him at all but that's not what he's there for, to please the crowd. Liverpool from the free kick have won the ball back in the middle of the field with Graham Souness. Plays it forward – a good ball – to Sammy Lee. Lee lays it on to Irwin. Irwin on to Dalglish, fifteen yards from the penalty area. Dalglish has to hold and check and turn and then play – a very unDalglishlike ball – but at least it found a Liverpool man, Lee, who has come all the way back into his own half to try and make some space. Thompson to Alan Kennedy. Alan Kennedy on to Dalglish. Dalglish takes it just inside the penalty area. Oh he's beaten one defender. Still has it. Places for McDermott, and it's headed off the line by Nicholl.

**Questions to think and talk about**

1  The two extracts are about the same football match. Where do you think each one comes from?
2  What are the differences between them that tell you this?

## Sentences in speech and writing

Sentences in writing and sentences in spoken language are very different. When we are speaking we don't usually think about this. We don't normally see our spoken sentences written down. When we do, they can look very strange.

SON: I took 40p and it only cost 30p.

FATHER: Hullo . . . that's all right . . . I've pinched your tape recorder.

SON: That's all right.

FATHER: You took for- . . . you did what? . . . you took for- . . .

SON: I took forty of it.

FATHER: Uh huh.

MOTHER: You took forty of what?

SON: 40p.

MOTHER: Of yours or Daddy's?

SON: Of Daddy's.

MOTHER: Oh. I see.

In conversation we have to make up our sentences as we go along. If people cannot understand, they can ask us to explain again. We can use our eyes as well as our ears to help us understand what is going on.

When we write, we have time to think and plan our sentences. The reader, however, only has the sentences on the page. He cannot usually ask the writer to explain things, because the writer is no longer there. So if you begin a piece of writing with this sentence:

I took 40p and it only cost 30p.

the reader cannot fully understand. He does not know what *it* is. In the conversation the father did know what *it* was. The son was holding *it*: a Sunday newspaper.

## Written sentences

Sentences in writing usually have a subject and a verb:

| Subject | Verb |
|---|---|
| A second goal | had to come. |
| A shot by Alan Kennedy | was deflected     to Irwin. |

## Spoken sentences

In speech, sentences have different rules. They are simply groups of words that make sense in the conversation:

Uh huh.

Of yours or Daddy's?

If we wanted to turn these spoken sentences into complete written sentences we should either have to change them completely, or at least add more words to them:

*Uh huh.* would become    *I understand.*

*Of yours or Daddy's?* would become    *Was the money yours or Daddy's?*

**Exercise 1**    The words that follow are part of the same football commentary as Extract B. Write the passage out in speech sentences as was done in Extract B. Begin each sentence with a capital letter and end it with a full stop. Add any other punctuation that is needed.

Well it's a Southampton throw and it'll be er in fact the linesman disagrees it's a Liverpool throw just immediately below us we're high up almost on the halfway line a superb position here at Anfield as Ray Kennedy gets a second throw playing it off the legs of er Nicholl again Southampton take it away from Liverpool then they give it away there's the most extraordinary clearance by Alan Kennedy and er Kennedy er Hanson in fact was challenged rather severely there by Keegan Hanson about six foot three and Keegan about five foot eight and Keegan went spinning into him so it'll be a free kick to Liverpool with now a quarter of an hour to go here Liverpool two Southampton nil so very important not only for Liverpool to win of course but to win convincingly

**Exercise 2**    Make a list of five sentences from Extract B that would not be complete as written sentences. Then reword each sentence to make it a complete written sentence.

*Example*: Alan Kennedy on to Dalglish.

*Rewritten*: Alan Kennedy passes the ball on to Dalglish.

**Exercise 3**    Extract A is a *report*. Extract B is a *commentary*. Write a short commentary and a short report on one of the following:

a school match (choose whatever sport you like)

a national tiddlywinks or conkers championship

boiling an egg

## *Your own writing*

Many people find that one reason that they make mistakes when they write is that they write as they speak. They write down sentences which would be correct in speech, but which are not complete in writing. The following passage contains examples of this type of mistake.

My hobby is keeping guinea pigs. Or cavies. Because that is their correct name. They aren't difficult to keep so long as you follow a few simple rules. They must be kept dry and warm. If it gets below sixty it doesn't do them any good. They need plenty of litter. I use sawdust. They need plenty of green vegetables. Like lettuce or cabbage. Mine like carrots too. They must be cleaned out regularly. At least once a week. You throw the old litter away and put in disinfectant. Let it dry. Then put the new litter in.

If this passage is read aloud, it sounds all right. As a piece of writing it is difficult to understand, because it does not follow the rules for written sentences. For example, *Or cavies* is not a complete written sentence. We need to rewrite the beginning like this:

My hobby is keeping guinea pigs, or cavies, which is their correct name.

**Exercise 4**    Rewrite the rest of the passage in complete written sentences.

# Moving from speech to writing

There are occasions when we need to turn a piece of speech into writing. An interviewer questions someone and then writes a report on it. A group has a discussion and then the members of the group have to report in writing on what they have decided.

## *The test*

This extract comes from a conversation between a teacher and two boys. They are talking about a Religious Education lesson.

GARETH: You see Mr ————— gave us a sort of study to do, in which he wrote out er –

MARK: A passage.

GARETH: A passage and either left blanks or said A B and C and you had to give him the right . . . well . . . we were arguing about . . . 'Well I think it's A' . . . 'No B' . . . 'No A' . . . and arguing like that.

TEACHER: What – these were sentences . . . with?

GARETH:
MARK: Yeah.

TEACHER: What was it about?

GARETH: It was . . . oh . . . Bible passages.

MARK: Yes: the leper in the temple and what Jesus said and –

GARETH: Yes.

MARK: He reckoned it was . . . What did you reckon it was?

GARETH: Oh yeah . . . I reckoned um . . . 'Get up and go'.

MARK: Yes.

GARETH: And he reckoned it was: 'Your faith has . . .

MARK: Healed.

GARETH: . . . has healed you.' That's right.

MARK: And it ended up: 'Your sins are forgiven.'

TEACHER: Which is the third one?

GARETH:
MARK: Yeah.

Exercise 1    In this conversation Gareth and Mark help each other out in remembering what happened. If the teacher now asked one of them to write a short description of what happened in the test, what would he write? Try to explain what happened in as few sentences as possible.

## Scrambling

This extract comes from an interview about a 6-year-old boy called Geoffrey, who has just started as a competitive motor-cycle scrambler. He is about to enter his first competition.

INTERVIEWER: Michael, you're Geoffrey's father. Isn't he a bit too young for this sort of thing?

FATHER: Well, he is very small. This is one of the problems. We've tried to get the smallest competitive bike that we could for him.

INTERVIEWER: Do these lads compete against lads their own age, or older lads?

FATHER: Well, it's in five groups, and he competes in the 6 to 7½-year-old.

INTERVIEWER: Geoffrey, what do you think of motor-cycling? When did you start?

GEOFFREY: Four years ago.

INTERVIEWER: Why did you start doing this?

GEOFFREY: Because I copied off me brother. It's good fun – starting off in a big line.

INTERVIEWER: And then what happens?

GEOFFREY: You've got to fight for your place.

INTERVIEWER: You've got to fight . . . fight for your place? What's the hardest thing, Geoffrey, about riding the bike?

GEOFFEEY: Changing gear.

INTERVIEWER: And what happens then?

GEOFFREY: Let your clutch out and then you start to move . . .

FATHER: He's picking it up quite well. He had an automatic bike before and this one . . . the competitive bikes've got gears and he is finding it a little bit harder . . . changing the gears.

INTERVIEWER: I suppose there are those that say that it's . . . er . . . it's maybe dangerous teaching young people to ride bikes at this age. Six years old.

FATHER: A lot of people say this, but when you go to a meeting and you actually see them riding there are . . . relatively few accidents on the track and usually it's just a broken leg or something which is . . . it's very rare you get a fatal accident in scrambling with . . . with schoolboys.

BBC Radio 4 *Today,* March 1981

Exercise 2     You are the interviewer and you have to write a report about Geoffrey for your local paper. Write a report of about 100 words giving the main facts. Give your report a suitable headline.

Exercise 3     Choose someone you know and interview him or her about a topic of interest. Either make notes on the interview, or – if you can – tape record it. Write a report on the interview.

# *Like . . . er . . . yeah*

Sometimes it is quite difficult to sort out the meaning of what someone has said. This is a conversation between John Lennon and Andy Peebles.

John Lennon:  How that record (*Whatever Gets You Through The Night*) came about was that Elton was in town and I was doing it and needed a harmony, he did the harmony on that and a couple more, and played beautiful piano on it, and jokingly he was telling me he was going to do this Madison Square Garden concert and he said, will you do it with me if the record's Number One? And I did not expect it to get to Number One at all. I didn't think it had a chance in hell. Well I said, sure, sure I would, sure I will. Well, I lived to get nervous about that because a year later or whenever it was, he came back and said, okay it's time to pay your dues.

Andy Peebles:   And the record went to Number One.

John Lennon:  Yeah, and it was the first Number One I had actually. *Imagine* wasn't Number One, *Instant Karma* wasn't Number one which I think were all better records than *Whatever Gets You Through The Night*, words are pretty good, but anyway so what could we sing? That was the point, so we sang Paul's song, *I Saw Her Standing There*. So I'm on Elton's record, but it was quite nice and that's when Yoko and I got back together the night I performed with Elton at Madison Square Garden. And I went on there and did the number and was quite astonished that the crowd was so nice to me, because I was only judging by what the papers said about me, and I thought I may as well not be around you know. And the crowd was fantastic.

*The Lennon Tapes:* BBC

Exercise 4    In a few simple sentences, explain what happened.

# What you say and how you say it

## *Record request*

These two extracts are both from record request programmes on BBC radio.

A     . . . And Sarah Green is 18 today. She's not going to the ————— Bank today because she's going to the dental hospital. Oh yes . . . heard it all before. Please wish her a very happy birthday from Mum, Dad, sister Cheryl, who's 13. Also wish her Great Aunt Dot a Happy Birthday, who's 21 again the same day. So that's for you to have a good time at the dental hospital – not that I don't believe for a moment. Eleven minutes to eight. Number 26 this week is New Entry Number 5: *Planet Earth* . . .

B     Now we continue with Your Midweek Choice and three pieces of music selected from the many, many letters and postcards we've received. First on the pile is Mozart's Oboe Quartet in F, Kochel number 370. Then comes a Motet by Mendelssohn, and finally we'll hear the Symphony number 10, *Antar* by Rimsky-Korsakov. First then the Mozart, which I'm playing for Monsieur Henri Grandet of Edgbaston, Birmingham. It's scored for oboe, violin, viola, and cello, and on this record it's played by . . .

**Questions to think and talk about**

1   These two programmes were aimed at different audiences. How would you describe the audience for each one?
2   Apart from the music chosen, how can you tell the kind of audience?
3   What effect does each speaker aim to have on his audience?
4   Judging from the words on the page, what do you think was the *tone of voice* of each speaker?

**Exercise 1**

In the next two extracts the speakers are again introducing pieces of music. Read them through and then write answers to the questions that follow.

C     This morning we have The Who and Police in performances from their latest recordings. But we begin with a well-loved song by John Lennon and Paul McCartney. The song, *She's Leaving Home* was composed over a period of some weeks during the time when the Beatles were compiling material for an album later to be called *Sergeant Pepper's Lonely Hearts Club Band*. It makes fairly elaborate and ambitious use of instrumentation and vocal backing, very much in keeping with the Beatles' style at this period . . .

D  . . . The L.P.O. and Beethoven's *Emperor Concerto* . . . er right now that seems to be about it . . . Yes, that about wraps it up. Pete's coming along in a few minutes with some Mozart and Haydn and things like that. I think that's just about all – just tidy the studio up a bit – vacuum the floor and so on. One more to go before we finish – the BBC Symphony Orchestra and Britten's *Spring Symphony* – and let's hope that for poor old Britain Spring *is* just around the corner! Oh yes, we know how to run a radio station here!

Questions to think and talk about

1  What kind of audience would be likely to listen to the music mentioned in extract C?
2  Who would be likely to listen to the music mentioned in extract D?
3  What is the *tone of voice* in extract C? Quote a sentence from it to show what you mean.
4  What is the tone of voice in extract D? Quote a sentence from it to show what you mean.
5  Do you think the tone is suitable in each case?
6  If not, rewrite one of the two extracts in a more appropriate tone.

## Royal engagement

These two news items are both taken from BBC radio. They come from different channels.

E  For Lady Diana Spencer, today sees the start of a whole new way of life, now that she's engaged to Prince Charles. To begin with she'll now have a personal detective wherever she goes, and her home until the wedding is with the Queen Mother at Clarence House. This morning Lady Diana is expected to meet her mother, Mrs Shand Kydd, who's due back in Britain after a holiday in Australia . . .

F  Lady Diana Spencer is beginning a new way of life today as Prince Charles' fiancée. After the announcement of their engagement, the couple spent yesterday evening at the Queen Mother's home, Clarence House, having dinner with the Queen Mother and Lady Diana's grandmother, Lady Fermoy. This morning Lady Diana is expected to meet her mother, who's due back in England, after a holiday in Australia.

**Questions to think and talk about**

**1** The two news items went out at exactly the same time. One was on BBC Radio 4, the other on BBC Radio 2. Which was which?
**2** Exactly *how* are they different?
**3** *Why* are they different?

**Exercise 2** Make up short news items about the following stories. In each case write *two* versions: one for a programme that is listened to mainly by people your own age, and the other for a programme for older people.

British Rail

NO TRAINS TONIGHT

Buffet & Bar

# What you write and how you write it

## Budget Day, March 1981

A   HOWE PICKS PAIN ALL ROUND

**Interest rates cut 2 per cent but 20p on petrol, beer up 4p**
by Ian Aitken, Political Editor
Sir Geoffrey Howe yesterday offered the country what may well be the grimmest spring Budget of any Government since the post-war-austerity days of Sir Stafford Cripps.

It was, he made clear, the deflationary price the country had to pay for his delivery of a 2 per cent cut in interest rates.

Besides swingeing increases in the duties on drink and tobacco, the Chancellor also imposed a 20p increase in petrol tax . . .

B   UP YOURS!

**Rude blow from Sir Tax-a-lot**
by John Desborough and David Thompson
The Chancellor had only one message for motorists, smokers, and drinkers yesterday – up yours.

UP goes your petrol by an explosive 20p a gallon.

UP goes your cigarettes by a choking 14p on a packet of 20.

UP goes your beer by a bitter 4p a pint.

UP goes your spirits by a snorter of 60p a bottle.

**Questions to think and talk about**

1   What kind of newspaper do you think each extract came from?
2   What makes you think that?
3   What is the *tone* of A? Can you quote a sentence to show this?
4   What is the *tone* of B? Can you quote a sentence to show this?

**Exercise 1**   Write down the answers to these questions.

1 a   Count the number of words in each extract (excluding headlines and the authors' names).
 b   Count the numbers of sentences in each extract.
 c   Write down the average number of words per sentence in Extract A. Do the same for Extract B.
2   Which extract contains more *facts* about the budget?
3   Which extract makes its writer's feelings about the budget clearer?
4   Look at your answers to questions 1, 2, and 3. What do they tell you about the two newspapers the extracts came from?

**Exercise 2**
1 Make a list of all the adjectives used in extract A.
2 Make a list of all the adjectives used in extract B.
3 Compare the two lists – does this tell you any more about the ways in which the two newspapers are written?

**Exercise 3** Make up short news reports about one of these two stories. Write *two* versions of the same story: one in the style of extract A and one in the style of extract B. Give each report a suitable headline.

# Types of writing: narrative and descriptive

When you are going to write about a subject, it is useful to know what kind of writing you want to do. Two of the commonest kinds of writing are *narrative* and *descriptive*.

A   Kestrels have pointed wings and long tails. These are the easiest ways to identify them. The adult male has wings which are a reddish brown on top, changing to a darker brown at the tips. The underside of the bird is a creamy-yellow colour. The adult female is marked with bars and streaks which make it look very different from the male.

B   A kestrel flew out of the monastery wall and veered away across the fields behind the farm. Billy knelt and watched it. In two blinks it was a speck in the distance; then it wheeled and began to return. Billy hadn't moved a muscle before it was slipping back across the face of the wall towards the cart track.

**B. Hines,** *Kes*

A is *descriptive* writing. It tells us what a kestrel *is like*.
B is *narrative* writing. It tells us what a kestrel *did*.

Very often, a piece of writing is not purely descriptive or narrative, but a mixture of the two:

C   Billy produced the sparrow from his bag and pushed it up between the finger and thumb of his glove. The hawk immediately pinned it with one foot and with her beak began to pluck the feathers from its head. Plucking and tossing in bunches, left and right, sowing them to the wind. Baring a spot, then a patch of puckered skin. She nipped this skin and pulled, ripping a hole in it and revealing the pale shine of the skull, as fragile and delicately curved as one of the sparrow's own eggs. Scrunch.

In this passage from the same book the author tells a story: about what the kestrel did. That is narrative writing. He also describes very vividly what the dead sparrow looked like. That is descriptive writing. Most stories contain a mixture of narrative and descriptive writing like this.

Exercise 1   For each of these extracts, state whether it is:
    **a**  mainly descriptive
    **b**  mainly narrative
    **c**  a mixture of the two

1    The rabbit had not seen him. He moved forward a step, hardly breathing. The animal turned its head and looked at him in alarm. He saw how its nostrils quivered and twitched. The eyes were very shiny and translucent. Kingshaw lunged forward suddenly, and fell upon the rabbit, pinning it to the ground.

2    There was a fair space of derelict ground between the old terrace and the wire fence round the school. It was good for playing, because the blokes who'd knocked down Jericho had left up lots of little bits of old wall, some of them quite high.

3    Bernard saw a flashing movement, at the same time as he heard a loud shout. He turned right to see the Shofiq lad come roaring out of the garden of an old dumpy house like an express train. He'd dropped the wallbrick and picked up something that looked like a length of old rubber hose. It was about ten feet long, and grey, and an inch thick. What's more, he was swinging it round his head, round and round, faster and faster, as he ran.

4    The sun was setting as they clambered on to the rim of the hills, and saw the country to southward stretching away in front of them, bathed in golden light: a magnificent panorama: a scene of primeval desolation: mile after hundred mile of desert, sand and scrub. And in the far distance, pools of silver; pools of glinting, shimmering light; pools that shivered and wavered and contracted, and seemed to hang a fraction above the horizon.
    The boy danced with delight.

Exercise 2   For each of these groups of words, state whether it is more likely to be useful in writing a narrative or a description. Explain why.
    **1**  hurried   stopped   gradually   then   fiercely
    **2**  engine   power   tyres   sleek   expensive
    **3**  swift   muddy   slime   crocodiles   dangerous
    **4**  stood   minutes   thinking   back   began   quickly
    **5**  glass   fragile   element   electricity   light

Exercise 3   Choose one of the groups of words in Exercise 2. Use all the words in the group to write a short description or a short narrative.

Exercise 4   Take the same group of words as you used in Exercise 3. Now write whatever you did not write last time. (e.g. If you wrote a description for Exercise 3, now use the same words in a narrative.)

**Exercise 5**    Choose two of these photographs. About one of them write a short *description*. About the other write a short piece of *narrative*.

# What kind of description?

The kind of description you write depends on *why* you are writing: who do you want to read what you have written? What effect do you want to have on your reader?

A **Sicilian Cyclamens**
Cyclamens, young cyclamens
Arching
Waking, pricking their ears
Like delicate very-young greyhound bitches
Half-yawning at the open, inexperienced
Vista of day,
Folding back their soundless petalled ears.

B **Cyclamen neapolitanum**
Like all cyclamen the petals are recurved and in this and several others of the autumn flowering group they have slightly bead-like auricles round the mouth of the flower and restricting it; in this species the mouth is not so much round as hexagonal. Each flower is about half an inch in height . . .

C **Cyclamen F¹ Hybrid Firmament Novelty!**
Beautifully proportioned plants with a wealth of flowers carried well above the neat, low foliage. The large blooms are in several distinct shades of pink; some with a dark red centre, salmon scarlet, rosy violet or pure white. This splendid type is now grown almost exclusively by leading florists and we highly recommend it.

**Questions to think and talk about**

1  How do the descriptions differ from each other?
2  How would you describe each type of writing?
3  What kind of reader is each one aimed at?
4  What is the purpose of each description?

**Exercise 1**  Draw three columns. Head them A, B, C. In each column list the adjectives used in that passage:

| A | B | C |
|---|---|---|
| young | recurved | neat |

and so on.

Look at the lists you have made. Pick one or two adjectives from each list. Explain why each is typical of the piece of writing that it came from.

**Exercise 2**  These two columns both contain adjectives which can be used to describe a car. Each column contains words which are more suitable for one type of description that another. Study the lists and decide what type of description each is suitable for.

| A | B |
|---|---|
| hydraulic | powerful |
| pneumatic | sleek |
| lubricated | roomy |
| electronic | inexpensive |

Now make up a similar pair of lists of adjectives to describe one of the following:

a TV set    an item of clothing    a drink

**Exercise 3**  Choose one of the photographs on the opposite page. Write two descriptions of it. Write each one for a different audience and with a different purpose.

Writing A: description suitable for a travel brochure
Writing B: description suitable for a school geography book

# What kind of narrative?

Like descriptions, narratives vary according to the *audience* and the *purpose* of the writing. They also depend on the *subject matter*. Each of these three passages is about a different subject studied in school. Words that may give a clue to what the subject is have been missed out.

A   As the . . . . . . reached its height, the two . . . . . . saw that neither side could win. The courage of the . . . . . . was so great, however, that neither . . . . . . nor . . . . . . was prepared to give way. They . . . . . . with . . . . . . , . . . . . . , and . . . . . . . Even sticks and stones were used in the desperate efforts of each side to . . . . . . the other. At last night fell and the battered . . . . . . made their way back exhausted to their . . . . . . .

B   The . . . . . . was filled with 5 . . . . . . of . . . . . . . A second . . . . . . was filled with 10 . . . . . . of . . . . . . . The . . . . . . in the first . . . . . . was then poured into the second . . . . . . . There was a small . . . . . . and . . . . . . . . . . . . was given off. This was . . . . . . and was observed to burn with a . . . . . . . . . . . . .

C   In this area there are three main . . . . . . . . . . . . . . , . . . . . . , and . . . . . . . The . . . . . . is extreme. During winter there is heavy . . . . . . and . . . . . . fall below zero. This means that it is impossible to . . . . . . . . . . . . . In summer very high . . . . . . are experienced. This makes it possible to . . . . . . . . . . . . . , . . . . . . , and . . . . . . . In recent years new advances have made it possible for the . . . . . . to get much higher . . . . . . by the use of new techniques. (See picture on page . . . . . . )

**Questions to think and talk about**

1   What subject does each piece of writing come from?
2   What makes you think this?
3   Can you work out what the exact subject matter of each piece is?
4   Do different subject teachers expect *you* to write in different ways?
5   If so, why is this?

**Exercise 1**   Here are three lists of words. They come from writing about the same subjects as passages A, B, and C on the last page. They are *not* necessarily the actual words missing from those passages.

| 1 | 2 | 3 |
|---|---|---|
| compound | region | general |
| substance | agriculture | forces |
| emitted | rainfall | century |
| acid | industry | campaign |

Which list belongs to which subject, and why?

**Exercise 2**   **a**   These two columns contain verbs which can be used to describe an explosion. Each column lists words which are more suitable for one school subject than another. Study the lists and decide which subject each is suitable for and why.

| 1 | 2 |
|---|---|
| charged | ignited |
| ordered | expanded |
| killed | reacted |
| destroyed | given off |

   **b**   These topics could be written about in more than one school subject:

a fight or conflict
making something
someone helping someone else

   i   Choose one of the topics.
   ii   Name two school subjects it might be written about in.
   iii   Make a list of at least four suitable verbs for each subject.

**Exercise 3**   Go through your own exercise books for different subjects. Concentrate on writing that is mainly *narrative*. Study the different ways you write narrative for different school subjects. Now write a few sentences explaining what you have found out.

# Points of view

A  Boy 1: That's mine!
   Boy 2: No it isn't.
   Boy 1: Yes it is. It's mine.
   Boy 2: No it's not.
   Boy 1: It's mine. Give it back!
   Boy 2: No.

B  Boy 1: That's mine!
   Boy 2: Who says?
   Boy 1: I do. My uncle gave it to me.
   Boy 2: Prove it.
   Boy 1: It was a birthday present. See – there's the date still marked
          on it. Give it back.
   Boy 2: No.

**Questions to think and talk about**

1  In what ways are these two conversations similar?
2  In what ways are they different?
3  In which conversation does Boy 1 make out a better case?
4  Why?

## *Written arguments*

Sometimes people have arguments in writing.

> Dear Sir,
>     I am writing to complain about the appalling state of the city's buses. They never seem to be swept out or washed. Frequently in the morning I have travelled on a bus that has obviously not been cleaned the previous night: with greasy chip papers and drink cans lying around all over the place. Considering how high the bus fares are these days, this sort of thing is quite disgusting.
>                         Yours faithfully,
>                         J.G. McBain

Dear Sir,

May I take this opportunity of answering Mr. McBain's letter last week about the city's buses. It is our regular policy to wash all buses twice a week and to sweep them thoroughly every night. Unfortunately during the past six weeks we have had severe staff shortages, due to illness. Nevertheless we have managed to keep our cleaning schedule up to about 90% of its normal standard. I am very sorry that Mr. McBain has been inconvenienced. I think he has also been unfortunate enough to travel on the 10% of buses that have recently been missing our usual thorough cleaning. I can assure him that we are doing the best we can in difficult circumstances.

Yours faithfully,
M.R. Rhodes
(General Manager, City Buses)

These two letters provide different different arguments, or points of view. In each case the writer gives the *reasons* for the point of view expressed. Especially in written arguments, this is very important.

If you only state your point of view and do not give any reasons, you will find that people do not take much notice of you.

Exercise 1    The following letter has appeared in your local paper. Write an answer to it.

Dear Sir,

I am appalled at the vandalism in our town. Everywhere you look there are windows broken, graffiti daubed on walls and telephone boxes smashed up. Young people have never had it so good and yet all they do to repay society is to destroy things. I think they ought to bring back corporal punishment for vandalism.

Yours faithfully,
H.L. Tudor

## *Why? . . . because*

Key words when expressing an argument are:

**why    because    therefore    since    as    so**

Exercise 2

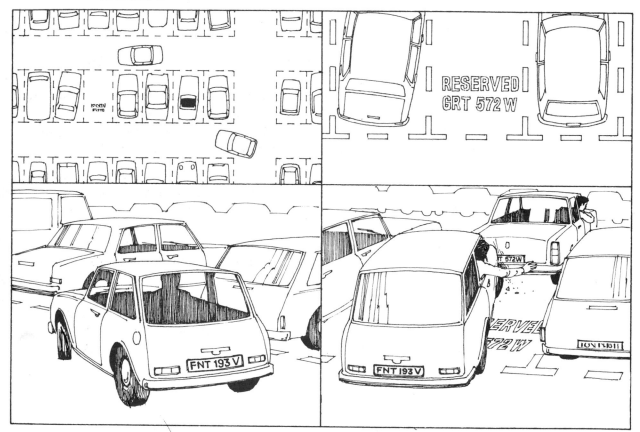

Each of these drivers thinks that the accident was the fault of the other driver. Write two statements, one by each driver explaining why *he* was in the right.

Exercise 3   **a**   Complete each of these sentences. Write each one down and leave a good space before you write the next one.

    i   If there's one thing I can't stand, it's . . .
    ii   The trouble with school is . . .
    iii  If I had my way I'd . . .
    iv  I can't bear people who . . .
    v   If I could, I'd ban . . .

  **b**   In the space after each sentence, write as many reasons as you can to back it up.

  **c**   Choose one of the sentences. Use what you have written as the basis of a clearly written and well argued composition on the topic.

# In brief

## *What does it stand for?*

'Here are the news headlines from ITN. The AA and the RAC report heavy congestion on roads out of London. UN members have attacked the USSR and the USA for lack of action over funds for UNESCO and UNICEF. The TUC has condemned Government plans to reduce staff in the DHSS and the HMSO. The death is announced of Sir Norman Grant, KCMG, DFC, MA.'

Abbreviations save time. It would be tedious to have to say or write 'The Automobile Association and the Royal Automobile Club', so we simply say 'The AA and RAC' and everyone knows what we mean. Often we know what an abbreviation *means* without knowing what the letters actually *stand for*. For example, you probably know what the letters **e.g.** mean – but what do they stand for?

**Exercise 1**  These abbreviations are all in common use. Write each one down. Against it, write what it means and what the letters stand for.

ITN  BBC  AD  BC  TUC  VC  i.e.  etc.  BA  USSR

## *Acronyms*

An acronym is a name made out of an abbreviation.

NATO  The North Atlantic Treaty Organization
ASH  Action on Smoking and Health

**Questions to think and talk about**
1  How many other acronyms can you think of?
2  What are the advantages of acronyms: why do people like to use them?
3  Suppose you had to start a group to do one of the things listed below. Can you think of a name to call it that would make a good acronym (like ASH)?
improve school meals
keep city streets tidy
provide more leisure activities in your district

e.g. stands for 'exempli gratia' in Latin

**Background knowledge**

Abbreviations are only useful as long as the people you are writing for, or speaking to, know what they mean. As we have seen, some are so commonly used that most people have heard them and have a general idea of their meaning. On the other hand some are less common. You may hear the initials GNP used on a TV news programme, but even if you are told that they stand for Gross National Product, you are probably not much the wiser. Similarly only an aircraft enthusiast is likely to know IAS (Indicated Air Speed) and a computer specialist DMA (Direct Memory Access). In the same way many organizations and groups of people have their own special abbreviations which other people do not know.

**Questions to think and talk about**

1  What abbreviations are commonly used in your school?
2  Which of these are special to your school?
3  Would it be possible for a stranger to work out what any of these special abbreviations mean?

**Exercise 2**

School subjects also often have specialist abbreviations. Think of the subjects you study at school. For as many of them as you can, make a list of their special abbreviations. Against each abbreviation, write what it means.

*Example*: Mathematics
         HCF   Highest Common Factor
         and so on . . .

## Titles and headlines

To some extent, book titles are similar to abbreviations. They give us a useful short way of referring to something that may be long and complicated. Instead of saying, 'I've been reading a book about travelling on the motorway and how you can go to interesting places and find good inexpensive food,' you can simply say, 'I've been reading *Just Off the Motorway*.' The title is convenient and short and sums up what the book is about.

Write one or two sentences explaining what you think each of these books is about:

The Lawbreakers
Ride Better and Better
The Complete Indoor Gardener
You and Your Back
Statistics in Action

Farm Your Garden
The Last Days of Hitler
The Healer's Art
Self-Help House Repairs Manual
How to Lose Weight Without Really Dieting

Other titles are chosen to attract our interest. They may be humorous, intriguing, or strange. Usually, however, they still give quite a strong clue about the book's subject matter.

Here are five book titles:

Policeman's Progress
Birds, Beasts and Relatives
How to Cheat at Housekeeping
Vet Behind the Ears
Supernature

**Questions to think and talk about**

1 What do you think is the subject matter of each book?
2 Why?
3 Why do you think each title was chosen?

**Exercise 3**  Make up suitable titles – serious or amusing – for books about these subjects.

a Travelling in Europe with little or no money.
b How to re-use materials and objects that are normally thrown away.
c How to build and operate a variety of simple electronic gadgets.
d An introduction to colour photography for beginners and people with little experience.
e Conjuring tricks that can be done with very simple equipment.
f How to make simple maps and how to understand street plans and motoring maps.
g Detailed advice and suggestions about designing and making model aircraft that fly.
h Detailed advice and suggestions about designing and making your own fashion clothes.
i Detailed lists and maps of places in Britain where strange, mysterious, and magical things are said to have happened.
j Sports and games that can be played or practised by one person without any expensive equipment.

**News headlines**

Like book titles, newspaper headlines are usually brief and sum up a piece of writing. Sometimes they give us a very good idea of what to expect when we read the article:

# Five missing after Navy helicopters collide

Sometimes we have to do a little guessing:

# Drugs fortune hunt in sea

Sometimes the headline writer sets out to puzzle or amuse us, to persuade us to read the article:

# Reservoir goes under

What do you think each of these headlines is about?

Boy soldiers in storm ordeal

England face tough test

Cliff boy's tragic battle

Typist gets her man

Attack by bear could help zoo

Monks aim to change habits

**Exercise 4**   Write a suitable headline for each of these news stories. Your headlines can be serious and straightforward, or they can set out to puzzle or amuse the reader.

**a**   A boy of 13 jumped into a canal and saved a three-year-old child who had fallen in while her mother wasn't looking.

**b**   A family of six has just returned to Britain after sailing round the world in a small boat. On their journey they were almost capsized three times: twice in storms and once by a whale.

**c**   A television newsreader is to be prosecuted for dangerous driving. He told police that he had to hurry because he was late for work.

**d**   The Queen is visiting Papua, New Guinea. She was welcomed by a large and enthusiastic crowd. They were so enthusiastic that police had to hold them back and force a way through for the royal procession.

**e**   Large areas of north-west England were blacked-out last night by a freak storm, which left several hundred thousand people without power for eleven hours.

## *Making notes*

Abbreviations, book titles and newspaper headlines are all written to be read and understood by other people. We also write messages 'in brief' to ourselves: to remind ourselves of things.

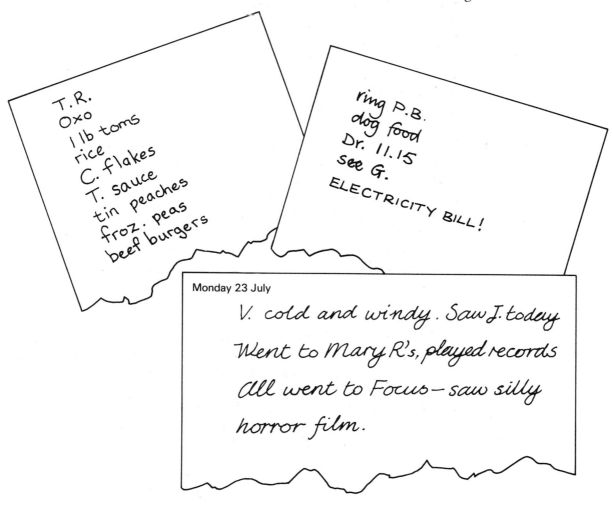

**Exercise 5**  **a** Choose one of the days in the past week. Write a diary of that day, describing the most important things that happened.
**b** Draw a rectangle 2 cm high by 6 cm wide.
**c** Now rewrite your diary entry, fitting it into the rectangle. Use any abbreviations you like – as long as *you* understand them.

**Exercise 6**  Choose a television programme that you have recently seen and enjoyed. You are going to tell the rest of the class about it. In preparation, make some notes for your talk, so that you do not forget anything important. Do not use more than four lines in your exercise book.

# Planning

| | |
|---|---|
| Think before you write | If you want to write effectively, you need to think before you write. You need to know the answers to a number of questions. |

What subject am I writing about?
What kind of writing is it to be?
Who will read it?
Why am I writing it?

Each question leads to further questions.

| | |
|---|---|
| What subject? | Is it set? |
| | How much choice is there? |
| | Do I understand the choice? |
| | Do I need more information? |
| | Where can I get information I need? |

| | | |
|---|---|---|
| What kind of writing? | Prose or poetry? | |
| | Narrative? | *see pp* 162 and 168 |
| | Descriptive? | *see pp* 162–7 |
| | Argument? | *see pp* 170–2 |
| | Script? | *see p* 185 |
| | Direct speech? | *see pp* 185–6 |
| | Letter? | *see pp* 182–3 |

| | | |
|---|---|---|
| Who will read it? | One person? | How well do I know him? |
| | | What does he expect? |
| | | What kind of reader is he? |
| | | What does he know about the subject? |
| | Several people? | Are they alike or different? |
| | | What do they have in common? |
| | | Do I know who they are? |
| | | How well do I know them? |
| | | What do they expect? |
| | | What do they know about the subject? |

| | | |
|---|---|---|
| Why am I writing? | To inform? | To amuse? |
| | To excite? | To persuade? |
| | To entertain? | To move? |
| | | Or why? |

# Getting it right

Most writing is done to communicate: to tell somebody something. If your writing is full of mistakes, you will not communicate very clearly. Most people make errors when they write. The good writer corrects his mistakes before saying he has finished.

A 3-point plan

**1** Read for meaning
Does it make sense?
Does it say what I mean?
Does it provide all the necessary information?
Will my reader(s) understand it?

**2** Check your sentences
Are they real sentences?   With a *subject and a verb*? *see p* 180
*Agreement*? *see p* 180
Do they begin with a *capital letter* and end with a *full stop*? *see p* 184
Have I put *commas* where they are needed?   *see p* 184
Is any *direct speech* correctly punctuated?   *see pp* 185–6

**3** Check your spelling
Are there any words I am not sure about?
Are there any words I often get wrong?   } Check in the dictionary
Are there any words I have not used before?

Are there any rules I often get wrong?   *see pp* 186–7

# Sentences and parts of speech

**Sentences**

There are three types of sentence: statement, question, and command.

**Statement:** Mary is at home.
**Question:** Where is Mary?
**Command:** Go home!

Sentences usually have at least a *subject* and a *verb*.

| subject | verb |
|---|---|
| Mary | is gardening |
| Who | spoke? |
| (you) | Stop! |

In commands the subject is 'you'. It is usually left out.
Some sentences have an extra part that tells us more:

| subject | verb | |
|---|---|---|
| Mary | is gardening | in the rain wearing gumboots. |
| Who | spoke | to her over the wall? |
| (you) | Stop | at once! |

The subject of the sentence may be *singular* or *plural*. Some verbs change according to whether the subject is singular or plural. This is called *agreement*.

Singular: *He* **is** champion of the world.
Plural: *They* **are** champions of the world.

Singular: *Mary* **goes** to a yoga class regularly.
Plural: *We* **go** for a walk instead.

**Parts of speech**
**Nouns**

Nouns are words used to name

**people:** woman  doctor
**places:** town  valley
**things:** trousers  record
**ideas:** hope  happiness

**Adjectives**

Adjectives qualify nouns. 'Qualify' means 'say more about'.
In this passage all the adjectives are in **bold** type.

Mr Gleeson had **round shiny** cuffs and **clean white** wrists and **fattish white** hands and the nails of them were **long** and **pointed**. *James Joyce*

**Verbs** Verbs are words used to describe **actions:** run hit
**states:** seem appear
**changes:** become grow

There are also auxiliary verbs. These work with other verbs. For example 'might' is an auxilary. We can combine it with 'go' in the sentence, 'I might go to Fulham tonight.'

The main auxiliaries are:
be am is are was were being been
has had have having
may might can could must ought
will shall would should do did

**Adverbs** Adverbs modify verbs, adjectives, or other adverbs. 'Modify' means 'say more about'. In this paragraph all the **adverbs** are in **bold** type.
The sound made me turn **quickly**. When I saw what had caused it, I stood **perfectly** still. The snake lifted its head **very slowly** and swayed **smoothly** from side to side, its eyes fixed **intently** in my direction.

**Pronouns** Pronouns are words used to stand instead of nouns. They save repetition.

| | |
|---|---|
| Personal pronouns: | I/me we/us he/him she/her you they/them |
| Impersonal pronouns: | it they/them |
| Possessive pronouns: | my our your his her their its |
| Relative pronouns: | who/whom which whose that |

# Letters

Writing letters to people you know

Setting out a letter

3 Fawcett Street
Oxford
OX4 3BW

1 Your address

4th May 1981

2 The date

Dear Mr Stevenson,

3 The greeting

I am recruiting parents
to help at this year's school sports
day. We need about twenty people
to supervise equipment and competitors.
Your daughter, Kate, told
my son, Mark, that you used to be a
keen amateur athlete, and I wondered,
therefore, if you would be interested in
helping. If so, I would be grateful if
you would let me know sometime this
week.

4 The letter

Yours sincerely,

5 The closing phrase

R. Macmillan

6 Your signature

Addressing the envelope

Mr J. Stevenson
120 Smethurst Road
ABINGDON
Oxon.
OX14 3JU

1 The person's title and name
2 Number and street
3 Post town in capitals
4 County
5 Postcode in capitals

Writing business letters

1 Your address

34 Elmwood Drive
Stopatham
Sussex
ST3 4BO

2 The title and address
of the person you are
writing to

The City Engineer's Department
Town Hall
Stopatham
Sussex

3 The date

3rd December 1981

4 The greeting
(usually 'Dear Sir')

5 The first paragraph
always says what
the letter is about

Dear Sir,
　　I am very dissatisfied with the way the road has been left by your workmen after the installation of new traffic lights in the High Street. It is so bumpy that I have been nearly shaken to pieces while riding my bicycle along it.
　　I think it quite likely that children riding at speed along the road could be jolted right off and injure themselves.

　　Please arrange for something to be done about this shoddy workmanship.

6 The closing phrase
(usually 'Yours
faithfully')

7 Your signature (initials
and surname)

Yours faithfully,
I. Harrison

# Punctuation

**Capital letters**  Capital letters are used:
1  To begin a sentence.
2  For the personal pronoun *I*.
3  For the main words in titles.
4  For days and months.
5  For names.
6  For initials.

**Full stops**  Full stops are used:
1  To end a sentence.
2  After initials.
3  After some abbreviations (except Mr Mrs Dr Revd Mme Mlle and names of very well known organisations e.g. BBC and AA)

**Commas**  Commas are used:
1  To separate the different things in a list.
   She packed only the most important items: towel, soapbag, nightdress, and clean underwear.

2  To mark off the first part of a sentence.
   After her husband died, she went away to live with her son.

3  To mark off the last part of a sentence.
   He did not even listen for Geoff's reply, if he made one.

4  To separate a group of words in the middle of a sentence.
   The island of Gont, a single mountain that lifts its peak a mile above the storm-racked Northeast Sea, is a land famous for wizards.

5  In direct speech. See page 185.

**Colons**  Colons are used:
1  to introduce a list.
   The fridge was full of food: pies, sausages, eggs, salad, and ice cream.

2  To introduce a saying, a statement, or an idea.
   The position was clear: either he tried to swim the river or he would certainly be caught.
   As the proverb says: a fool and his money are soon parted.

| | |
|---|---|
| **Apostrophes –**<br>**Omission** | Apostrophes are used to show where one or more letters have been missed out. |

we have  becomes  **we've**  who is  becomes  **who's**
are not  becomes  **aren't**  they are  becomes  **they're**

**Possession**

Apostrophes are used to show possession – to show that something belongs to someone or something.

1  We add **'s** to words that do not end in s.
  **John's** bike    **women's** rights
2  If a word already ends in s, we just add **'**.
  the **girls'** mother    **James'** friend

**its/it's**
its = of it    it's = it is

**Script**

Script is the way in which conversation is written down in plays.

[5](A crowded transport cafe. We see MIKE approach the table where the DRIVER is sitting.)
[1]MIKE:[3]  ([6]Anxiously)  [4]Excuse me . . .
[2]DRIVER:  (Bored) Yeah?

1  Put the name of each speaker in capital letters.
2  Put all the names underneath each other.
3  Put a colon after the name of each speaker.
4  Write the words spoken, *without inverted commas*.
5  Put instructions for the actors in brackets and underline them. If they are for all the actors, take a full line.
6  If they are just for the actor who is speaking, put them at the beginning of the speech.

**Direct speech**

Direct speech is the way in which conversations are written down in stories.

Mike went into the transport café. It was very crowded. He saw a lorry driver sitting alone in one corner and made his way across to him. He felt very nervous.
'Excuse me,' he began.
'Yeah?' said the driver in a bored voice. 'What do you want?'
'Could you give me a lift?'

1  The words spoken are always put in inverted commas: single – '. . . . . .'    or double – ". . . . . ."
2  Each new piece of speech begins with a capital letter.
3  Each piece of speech closes with one of these: **,    .    ?    !**

4 If you put the *he said* words before the speech, put a comma before the inverted commas:
He said, '. . . . . . . . . . . .'

5 If you put the *he said* words in the middle of a piece of speech, follow them with a comma or a full stop:
'. . . . . . . . . . .,' he said, '. . . . . . . . . . .'
*or* '. . . . . . . . . . .,' he said. '. . . . . . . . . . .'

6 If you follow the *he said* words with a full stop, the next piece of speech must begin with a capital letter.
'Yeah?' said the driver in a bored voice. '**W**hat do you want?'

7 Otherwise a capital letter is not needed there.
'I'm sorry,' he said, '**b**ut I've got to go.'

8 Every time there is a new speaker, start a new line and start writing about 1 cm in from the margin.

# Spelling: rules

1 **Long and short vowels**

Long: d*a*te prec*e*de l*i*ne j*o*ke *u*se
Short: p*a*d h*e*m r*i*p r*o*b c*u*t
Adding –ing and –ed: date dating dated
                                pad padding padded

2 **ie/ei**

Rule: 'i before e except after c when the sound is long ee'.
ie: field believe
ei: receive ceiling

Exceptions: seize weird

3 **-ly**

We add –ly to adjectives to make them into adverbs.

**a** With most words, just add -ly: bad badly
**b** for words that end in –l still add -ly: technical technically
**c** For words that end in –ll add -y: full fully
**d** for words that end in –y, change the -y to -i and then add -ly: funny funnily

4 Words that end in -y

  **a** If you add -s to a word that ends in -y, the spelling usually changes. The -y changes to -ie-: fry fries
  **b** If it is a verb that you make past by adding -ed a similar thing happens: fry fried
  **c** If you add -ing, you do not change the -y: fry frying
  **d** If the letter before the -y is a vowel, it does not change to an -i-: sway sways swayed
  **e** There are three exceptions to **d**:
  lay becomes laid
  pay becomes paid
  say becomes said

5 Plurals

Plural means more than one. Most words follow these rules.

  **a** Normally just add -s: head heads
  **b** With words that end -s, add -es: cross crosses
  **c** With words that end -ch, add -es: church churches
  **d** With words that end -f, change the -f to -ve: knife knives
  **e** With words that end in -y see rule above.

6 -er, -ar, -or

To make certain verbs into nouns we add -r or -er.

announce    announcer
photograph  photographer

There are other words that end with the same sound as -er, but are spelled differently. These just have to be learned. The commonest are as follows:

| ar | | or |
|----|----|----|
| beggar | liar | conductor |
| burglar | particular | editor |
| calendar | peculiar | doctor |
| circular | cellar | visitor |
| familiar | popular | instructor |
| regular | vinegar | bachelor |

7 -ful -fully

If we add -full to a word, it becomes -ful. If we then add -ly, it becomes -fully.

help + full = helpful
helpful + ly = helpfully

# Acknowledgements

The publishers would like to thank the following for permission to reproduce photographs:

Ardea Photographics, pp. 10, 163, 165; Barnaby's Picture Library, pp. 9, 19, 26, 42, 47, 71; BBC Hulton Picture Library, pp. 24, 69; British Tourist Authority, p. 165; Camera Press, pp. iv, 1, 71, 83, 96, 148, 157, 159, 165; J. Allan Cash, p. 113; Fay Godwin, pp. 35, 41, 42, 53; Gerald Friedlander, p. 1; Richard and Sally Greenhill, p. 71; Mr and Mrs Herman, p. 25; John Hillelson/Ian Berry/Magnun, pp. 1, 19; Alan Hutchison Picture Library, p. 22; Illustrated London News, p. 83; Imperial War Museum, p. 13; Italian Tourist Board (ENIT), p. 113; Keystone Press Agency, pp. 19, 71, 84, 87, 157; Mansell Collection, pp. 83, 84; National Film Archive, p. 97; Network, p. iv; Oslo/Munch Museum, p. 55; Pegasus Productions, p. 68; Pitkin Pictorials, p. 62; Portuguese Tourist Board, p. 124; Popperfoto, pp. 19, 71, 162; Spectrum Colour Library, p. 19.

Cover transparency courtesy of ZEFA/Armstrong

*Illustrations by:* Chris Molan, Tony Morris, David Watson, Freire Wright

The publishers would like to thank the following for permission to reprint copyright material:

BBC: for permission to reprint excerpts from news bulletins and record request programmes from Radio 1, Radio 2, Radio 3 & Radio 4 (See pages 150, 152, 155, 156, 157, 158.)    Ray Bradbury: 'The Pedestrian' from *The Golden Apples of the Sun*, Copyright © 1951 by The Fortnightly Publishing Company, copyright © renewed 1979 by Ray Bradbury. Reprinted by permission of the Harold Matson Company, Inc.    Melvyn Bragg: extract from Melvyn Bragg's interview with Joe Bill Lightfoot from *Speak for England*. Reprinted by permission of Martin Secker & Warburg.    John Braine: from *Room at the Top* (Eyre & Spottiswoode, 1957). Reprinted by permission of David Higham Associates Ltd.    Alan Brownjohn: 'To See the Rabbit'. First published in *The Railings* (Calder, 1961). Reprinted by permission of Macmillan, London & Basingstoke.    Charles Causley: 'In Coventry' from *Collected Poems* (Macmillan). Reprinted by permission of David Higham Associates Ltd.    Central Board of Finance of the Church of England: for permission to reproduce extracts from the Marriage Service of the *Alternative Service Book 1980*.    John Clare: 'I Am'. Copyright © Eric Robinson 1967. First published by Oxford University Press in *Selected Poems and Prose of John Clare*, chosen and edited by Eric Robinson and Geoffrey Summerfield. Reprinted by permission of Curtis Brown Academic.    Collins English Dictionary: definition of 'Holiday' reprinted by permission of the publisher.    Len Deighton: from *Bomber* (1970). Reprinted by permission of Jonathan Cape Ltd., for the author. Geoffrey Dutton: 'The Wedge-Tailed Eagle' from *Australian Short Stories of Today* (Faber). Reprinted by permission of the author.    Eyre & Spottiswoode (Publishers) Ltd: for permission to reprint extracts from *The Book of Common Prayer of 1662*, (Crown copyright).    Thom Gunn: 'Blackie, the Electric Rembrandt' from *My Sad Captains*. Reprinted by permission of Faber & Faber Ltd.    Woody Guthrie: 'Pretty Boy Floyd' from *The Folk Songs of North America* (comp. Alan Lomax, Cassell 1970). Paul Henley: from *Amazon Indians*. Reprinted by permission of Macdonald & Co. (Publishers) Ltd.    Barry Hines: from *Kes* (1968). Reprinted by permission of Michael Joseph Ltd.    Ted Hughes: extracts from pp. 15–20 and 56–61 of *Poetry in the Making*. 'The Thought Fox' from *The Hawk In the Rain*; 'View of a Pig' from *Lupercal*; 'Leaves', 'There Came a Day' and 'Work and Play', all from *Season Songs*. 'A Memory' and 'Hands' from *Moortown*. All reprinted by permission of Faber & Faber Ltd.    James Joyce: from *Portrait*

*of the Artist as a Young Man,* Reprinted by permission of Jonathan Cape Ltd., on behalf of the Executors of the James Joyce Estate.    Camara Laye: from *The African Child* (Fontana 1959). Reprinted by permission of Collins Publishers.    Lennon & McCartney: 'She's Leaving Home' by John Lennon and Paul McCartney © 1967 Northern Songs Limited for the World. All rights reserved.    Roger McGough: 'My busconductor', Copyright © Roger McGough 1967, from *Penguin Modern Poets* 10 (1967). 'Newsflash', Copyright © Roger McGough 1976 from *In the Glassroom* (Cape). Reprinted by permission of Tessa Sayle.    James Vance Marshall: adapted from *Walkabout* (1959). Reprinted by permission of Michael Joseph Ltd.    Christopher Middleton: 'Navajo Children' from *Nonsequences* (Longman 1965). Reprinted by permission of the author.    Bill Naughton: 'Rainbow' from *The Bees Have Stopped Working* (Wheaton 1976). Reprinted by permission of the author.    Robert O'Brien: from *Mrs Frisby and the Rats of NIMH* (1972). Reprinted by permission of Victor Gollancz Ltd.    The Observer: 'My happiest holiday' by David Garnett from *The Observer,* 30 December 1979; 'A Menace to Society' from *The Observer,* 11 June 1972. Copyright The Observer Ltd. Reprinted with permission.    George Orwell: from *England Your England*. Reprinted by permission of A. M. Heath & Co. Ltd., for the Estate of the late George Orwell, and Martin Secker & Warburg Ltd.    N. Postman & C. Weingartner: from *Teaching As A Subversive Activity* (Delacorte Press, 1969).    Hans Peter Richter: 'The Teacher (1934)' from Hans Peter Richter: *Friedrich*, trans. Edite Kroll (Kestrel Books, 1975) pp. 59–64. Copyright © 1961 by Sebaldus-Verlag G.m.b.H., Nurnberg; © 1970 by Holt, Rinehart & Winston, Inc. Reprinted by permission of Penguin Books Ltd.    Carl Sandburg: 'Circles' from *The People, Yes* by Carl Sandburg, copyright 1936 by Harcourt Brace Jovanovich, Inc., copyright 1964 by Carl Sandburg. Reprinted by permission of the publisher.    Vernon Scannell: 'Gunpowder Plot' from *A Mortal Pitch*. Reprinted by permission of the author.    Alan Sillitoe: from *A Start in Life*, © 1970 by Alan Sillitoe. Reprinted by permission of W. H. Allen & Co.    Henry Slesar: from 'Examination Day'. Reprinted by permission of the author's agent, Campbell Thompson & McLaughlin Ltd.    John Steinbeck: from *The Pearl* (1949). Reprinted by permission of William Heinemann Ltd.    Paul Thompson: extracts from *The Children's Crusade* (1975). Reprinted by permission of Heinemann Educational Books Ltd.    Kurt Vonnegut: from 'Tomorrow and Tomorrow and Tomorrow' from *Welcome To the Monkey House* (1968). Reprinted by permission of Jonathan Cape Ltd., for the author.    Keith Waterhouse: from *Mondays, Thursdays* (Michael Joseph). Reprinted by permission of David Higham Associates Ltd.    Arnold Wesker: extract from *I'm Talking About Jerusalem*, from *The Wesker Trilogy*. Reprinted by permission of Jonathan Cape Ltd., for the author.    Yevgeny Yevtushenko: 'Schoolmaster' from *Selected Poems* (Pergamon, 1963).

*Page 160*  'Howe picks pain all round' from *The Guardian*, 11 March 1981 'Up Yours!' is from the *Daily Mirror*, 11 March 1981.
*Page 165*  'Sicilian Cyclamens' is by D. H. Lawrence.  'Cyclamen neopolitanum' is from *Collins Guide to Bulbs* by P. M. Synge (1961). 'Cyclamen F1 Hybrid Firmament Novelty!' is from Dobie's Seed Catalogue 1981.